Melvyn Williams spent most of his childhood in
Goldenhill and Tunstall, Stoke-on-Trent, Staffordshire,
England and shares his lifelong memories of this in
'Just A Bloke From Stoke'

Contents

FOREWARD

We all have a story to tell but very few of us find the courage, determination, and time to dig deep and write a memoire. Because of this, I have no hesitation in endorsing 'Just a bloke from Stoke'
which shares, chronologically, the author's memories of growing up in the potteries, particularly in and around Goldenhill and Tunstall. The writer's unique, down-to-earth style is rather like sharing a cuppa and a chat with him, whilst turning the pages of a well-worn, lifelong, photograph album.

Vivien Jones
Author – Buried Tears

In 2012 on a snowy January morning, I started daydreaming about my youth. It was nothing special, in fact I would imagine that it was like most Baby Boomers. Recently, I was talking to one of our grandchildren about when I was roughly her age [12] and how life was so much different than it is today. I don't know if you have any grandchildren, and if you do, have you ever tried to talk to them about your past, and noticed a glazed look appear in their eyes! Bless her, she was trying to be polite and seem interested, but the reality was, that she just wanted to get back to her I Phone and see how many 'Likes' she had got from her last post.

This got me thinking about how I wish I had asked my parents, or grandparents about their lives before I was born. I thought, when we are gone, she will probably say, 'Oh I wish I had asked this or that. So, I decided to make some notes about my life. It was going to be just a few A4 pages, perhaps 3 or 4 and I thought that would cover it. Then it would be put into a folder, and if the time came that they wanted some answers, at least they would have something.

It didn't take me long to realise I had far more pages and photographs than I had anticipated. I thought that putting it into a book would make it far more accessible. Start at the beginning, I thought, a little about my parents and grandparents would give an idea of my background. Then move onto my school life and being a teenager in the wonderful 1960's, onto the 70's and marriage and on it went. I found it easier to put it into short stories rather than just a few dates and names, then I added the odd photo to go along with the story. I'm sure that many of you who were born just after WW2 and even into the early 60's will recognise my memories as similar to your own. I have lived all my life in the Stoke-on-Trent area, and feel pride in saying that. Outsiders have the impression that Stoke is not the best place to live, they only see the view put out by the media, but our little part of England has beautiful countryside equalling any other part of our green and pleasant land. Stoke-on-Trent is primarily made up of 6 towns that sit from Tunstall in the North to Stoke in the South, with many villages filling in the gaps between the towns. The area is mostly famous for its quality pottery that the rest of the world can only be envious of, hence the 6 towns are collectively known as the potteries, with names like Wedgwood and Doulton. Also, Reginald Mitchel the inventor of the Spitfire, and not forgetting James Brindley, the engineer of the canal system that revolutionised transport in the 18th century, are all part of the history of my wonderful City.

My life started at ten past nine on Monday morning the 8th August 1949 at the Haywood Hospital. I know this as a fact, because my mum told me so! Many years later, when I was much older and had left home, my mum and dad would ring me up at that precise time and sing happy birthday to me. The Haywood Hospital is situated around the area of Burslem, known as the Mother Town of Stoke-on-Trent. My mum was 21 when she had me, she was the youngest of three which was quite a small family for the time. The infant mortality rate was much higher than today, but the lack of any real form of family planning usually made for much larger families. My dad was 27 when I was born, and he was the eldest of 6, with two brothers and three sisters, they lived in an area of Stoke-on-Trent called Smallthorne. My dad's father left the marital home when all the siblings were quite young, leaving my paternal grandma to bring up all 6 children on her own. She did the best she could, working many hours to keep the family together. Considering that this was the 1930's with no financial help

5

from any Government body, made her efforts even more remarkable. The alternative would have been the Workhouse. Even though my paternal Grandad had left the family home, he lived close by. He had a shop selling groceries, and he was also one of the first in our city to open a petrol station. He dug out the holes that would house the petrol tanks by hand, which, was a mammoth task. The petrol station was next to the marital home, so you can see that even though he wasn't living with the family, he was working daily very close to them. I was never told why they had separated, but the hard work my grandma was forced to do to keep her children together, took its toll, and she died in her 40's. By this time my dad, along with the eldest sister, had started to work, so this helped to keep everyone together. Eventually my grandfather moved back in with his children. I could never understand why or how they forgave him, but not knowing all the facts, who am I to judge?

My paternal grandma and grandad. The back of the photo says it was taken in 1912. Arthur Bourn Williams, Mary (Polly) Williams nee Beech. It looks like they were at a wedding with the carnation in his lapel, but I don't think they were married at this time, as I can't see a wedding ring on my grandma's finger. No one seemed to smile back then when having their photo taken.

Not a lot happened in my birth year, the George Orwell book 1984 was published, as was Thomas the Tank, a children's book. Twiggy, a 1960's model and Mark Knopfler, who was a fabulous guitarist, were both born in 1949.

WW2 had only ended 4 years previously, but it took until the year of my birth for the rationing of clothes to come to an end.

A small black disc was also introduced to the public, even though it would take 12 years or so for this black disc to have a massive impact on my life. It had a very unimpressive name; they called it a 45, which was designed to be placed on a rotating platform with an arm and a needle resting on the grooves in the disc, and, like magic, you could play the music of your choice in your own home. The name 45 came from the revolutions that the disc made per minute.

At the time of my birth, many women would have their babies delivered at home, and would very often have a neighbour who would be called in to assist with the birth. The neighbour helping with the delivery could be the one chosen quite simply because she had had one or more babies herself and was therefore deemed to be "Experienced". My lifelong friend, who was born in 1950, the year after me, was one of those babies who was born at home. Well, I say at home, his parents lived in a house that didn't have an indoor water supply. So, when the time came, his mother went to the house next door to my maternal grandparents, to have her baby, quite simply because they had an indoor tap! "Get me some boiling water and some towels" seems to have been the request when a baby was imminent, if only it was that simple in that era.

In 1948 the NHS was born {pardon the pun} so my mum had a choice, and chose to go into Hospital for my imminent arrival. How Brilliant was that? She had the opportunity of free medical assistance with all the modern technology available. Apparently, my delivery was without any complications, having said that, my mum and I spent 10 days in Hospital, not that there was anything wrong, 10 days was normal at that time. [Now, mums can deliver their babies and be back home in just a few hours]. To visit us in

Hospital my dad would finish work at 5 o'clock and make his way home to my maternal Grandparents' house, where my parents were living at this time. After getting changed he then would have to catch two buses to the Hospital, the visiting time was 7 to 8pm, then afterwards make his way back home. I would imagine after 10 days of visiting us, my dad was looking forward to us coming home. Before I take you to my first home, I recently found a letter that my mum sent to my dad from Hospital just a few hours after I was born, it referred to the help that one of the Midwives at the time was giving to new mums. The midwife insisted, that if I wasn't taking my milk that my mum should slap my leg, and this would encourage me to concentrate and feed, just imagine how horrendous that was. My mum did try to tap my leg, but just couldn't bring herself to slap it!

Anyway after 10 days we were released from Hospital and sent home. Home being an end terraced house that we shared with my maternal grandparents, obviously, I didn't realise at the time, but I was so lucky to have had such a wonderful place to start my life. Not only did I have the countryside on my doorstep, but I had the most wonderful play park right outside the back gate

Unfortunately, I don't have many memories of my maternal grandparents, but there was one silly thing that stuck with me. I went into the posh room, you know the one, it was the room only used for special occasions. Well, I don't think my grandad cared much for the title given to this room. He was sitting at the table with all sorts of things spread over it, and as I walked in, he leaned forward and picked me up and sat me on his knee. I was fascinated with the two candles flickering on the table, and my grandad picked up a magnifying glass and put it in front of his eye, moving it forward and back, making his eye look bigger and smaller just to make me laugh. Someone knocked on the front door

9

and as my grandad opened it, still holding me in his arms, I remember a man standing there with a funny hat on. That little memory stayed with me, and many years later I mentioned it to my mum, she told me that her dad would repair watches to earn a bit of extra money, and the man with the funny hat would have been the local policeman, who would be there to collect his watch. A silly memory, but sadly the only memory I have of my grandad.

At the age of 5 you start to retain a few memories. My grandma would look after me when my mum and dad were at work. We had no pre-school then, so to entertain me she would do simple things like turn the clothes horse upside down, put a bed sheet over it, and hey presto, you had a tent. Things must have been looking up for my dad as he bought his first car, it was a Wolseley 14/60, and a week's holiday was also booked at Butlins, Skegness. We arrived on the Saturday for our first family holiday, but sadly, and within a few hours of our arrival, a message was sent to Butlins, my maternal grandad had died, so back home we went. Shortly after this my parents were offered a council flat on a big new estate, this was my parents dream, their own home. It was now 1954, and I was 5 years old.

We moved into 46 Westbourne Drive, Tunstall, it was at the very top of a new council estate. There were many houses on this estate, but our new home was a 2 bedroomed flat, each block had two flats on the ground floor and two flats above them, they basically looked like a large house divided into 4. We felt quite posh, not only did we have a bathroom but we had a boiler behind the coal fire that gave us hot water. It also had a front garden and a very large back garden, although, the gardens had to be shared with the flat below us.

I've mentioned, that when talking to our grandchildren about comparing our childhood to their own, that a glazed look might appear in their eyes, well this next story was the exception.

Our granddaughter came home from school and told us that they had a lady talking to them on Zoom, this was in 2021 when we were going through the Covid pandemic. The lady talking was a survivor of the Holocaust. It must be a difficult subject for young children to listen to, but like Remembrance Day, I think it's important that we never forget.

The conversation then moved on to what it was like when we were her age [13] in 1963, I said, well, when we were your age, the winters seemed to be much worse; "like what?" she asked. Well, it snowed a lot more. "Oh" she said, "I wish it would snow, I love snow". Like all kids today she had her phone permanently stuck to her hand, so I said to her "Google the winter of 1963". Her fingers were like grease lightning on her phone, and her eyes opened wide at the results she saw. "Wow, I wish it would snow like that now! "Well," I said, "we only have to have an inch of snow now and they close your School." "What's an inch?" she asked. So, I sort of showed her with a gap between my thumb and forefinger to show what an inch was. Then I said, "back in 1963 the snow was 6 feet deep!" "What's 6 feet?" she asked. "Well, it's about as tall as me!" her eyes widened again. Then I said, "and also, our school never closed!" "What !! she said, "they didn't close?" "No, and we had to walk to school!" Then I said, "when we woke up there were times when we could scrape the ice off the inside of our bedroom window!" "Why didn't you just turn the heating up? she asked. "What heating?! We only had a coal fire that had to be lit every morning and that was the only heat we had. Also, when I got home from school in winter the house would be freezing cold, and I would have to light the fire with paper and sticks of wood! and I had to

11

make sure that the wood was well alight before I put the coal on, but we were lucky!" "You were lucky? Why were you lucky?" "Well, we had moved into a council flat, and behind our fire we had a tank of water that was connected to the taps in the kitchen and bathroom, so when the fire was lit it warmed the water so we could have hot water. We were also lucky because we had electricity, so we could just switch the lights on! I said that before we moved into our council flat, we had gas lights!" Gas lights?! What are they?" I said, "google gas lights." Her fingers went to her phone again and she said, "How did they work?" Well, I struggled at this point, and said that they had a gas mantle, and you turned the gas on and lit the mantle, and it gave off light, also, you know the street lights outside that just come on when its dark? Well, before electricity they had to have someone who went to every lamp post to turn on the gas and light it!" This blew her mind and she said: "So, someone had to light every one?" "Yes, and not only that, every morning they had to turn them off." Then, Pat said to her," they also had someone who went to peoples' houses with a long stick who would knock on their bedroom window to wake them up for work!" "Well," she said, "who woke up the person who knocked on the window?" How do you answer that one?!"

She then told us that whilst at school, they had been shown the footage of our Queen's Coronation in 1953 and she surprised me by saying, "but you won't remember that, because you would only have been 4." Now, that did impress me. Pat told her, that on the Queen's Coronation, hardly anyone had a TV, and televisions back then, were only about 14 inches square. I think you can imagine what her next question was, ."what is 14 inches?" So Pat sort of gestured what 14 inches looked like. "Couldn't they just make them bigger?" I tried to explain to her that the

12

television pictures were made up of lots of lines. In fact, there were 405 lines and then, in the 1960s, they increased the lines to 625 and that was how they could make the TVs bigger. I knew I was digging a hole with all this talk about lines, but after my best efforts, I think I explained how the number of lines worked on the picture quality. She may have been just feeling sorry for me, but she just nodded her head as if to say, ok, if you say so. This was the conversation we had with our granddaughter, and I must thank the school for sparking the interest that started our little talk about growing up in the 1950s/60s compared to today. If in the future, our grandchildren, or maybe even their children, would like to know a bit about our lives they may think, well, they didn't have much, but what they did have was a bloody good time.

The black Disc that played a big part in my life in the 1960s, even though I would never have anything to play it on!

My dad with his first car. The back of the photo says, 1953 aged 32, Wolseley Hornet, colour green, 1934 model

The letter below is the one that my mum sent to my dad from hospital on the day I was born. It mentions how the ward Sister told her to smack my leg.

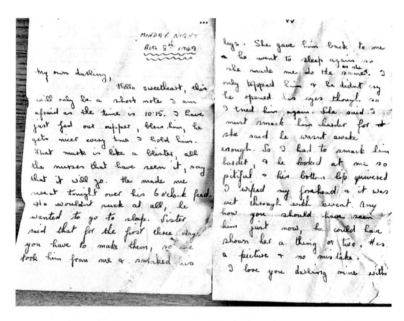

In part of this letter my mum also says, quote, [over his 6 o'clock feed he wanted to go to sleep. The sister said that for the first 3 days you must make them feed, so she took him from me and smacked his leg. She gave him back to me, but he went to sleep again, so she made me do the same as she did. I could only bring myself to tap his leg, he didn't cry, but he opened his eyes, so I tried to feed him again, she said I must smack his leg harder as he wasn't awake enough. So, I had to smack him a little harder, he looked at me so pitifully, and his bottom lip quivered].

15

Below, my dad introducing me to the play park, I was 10 days old, and the day mum and me came out of hospital.

This is a snapshot of a film the BBC would play if they had to fill in the gap between programs in the 1950s/60s. It was just simply a man throwing a lump of clay onto the potter's wheel, then forming it into a vase. I just thought this little snippet of Television nostalgia was fitting, considering this book is mostly about the potteries. [I wonder how many of you Baby Boomers remember this?]

BACK TO 1953

The bathroom in our new flat with hot running water was a step up from the tin bath that would be hung up in the back yard of our terraced house, it had to be dragged in and usually put in front of the fire. We had a boiler in the kitchen that you could light a fire under it to warm the water, and then a bucket full at a time would be poured into the tin bath. I think the Romans, two thousand years ago, had far better bathing facilities than we did in the 1950s but then again, thankfully, we didn't have slaves to provide such opulence as they did. I think the best thing was having an indoor toilet. The terraced house we had moved from had the toilet half way down the yard. In winter it was freezing and in summer the smell didn't encourage you to linger, and if you felt the need to go in the middle of the night you would use the pot that was put under the bed ☺

We had gone from living in our village of Goldenhill, where everyone knew each other, and there was a good variety of shops on the high street, and what seemed to be a pub every 100 yards, we even had our own cinema!

One of my memories at 5 years old was getting on a bus with my grandma which took us to Hanley, the biggest shopping centre in our city. We went to a pet shop, and after a lot of pointing, we both agreed the little puppy with the black patch over one eye was the one. Back at the bus stop, my grandma put our new family member into her shopping bag, and, whispered to me that dogs were not allowed on busses, so, we spent our trip back home hoping that no yapping came from her bag. We made it home and Lassie became my new little mate. I think my grandma just wanted some company after my grandad had died, and now that we had moved into our new council flat. Lassie had been with us for about two weeks when we started to realise that she was deaf, but over the years she turned out to be a really loving dog.

My grandma would visit us, and on one of these visits, I was in bed and heard a noise, I got up and went to see what it was, apparently, my grandma had knocked a cup of tea on the floor and it splashed up the wall. Years later my parents were decorating, and as they scraped the old paper off, my mum noticed the tea stain on the old wallpaper and started to cry, it's strange how silly little memories like these can stay with you.

Top photo, Lassie with me in the back garden of our new council flat. Bottom photo, Lassie, posing for her photo in the living room of my maternal Grandparents home. After my grandma died, we adopted her.

My maternal grandad holding me in his arms, as he did in
the story of the man with the funny hat.

My maternal Grandma with me taking the comfy option in the back yard of their house.

When I look at these photographs, I just wish that my memory could have retained the images, times, and places.

TIME FOR SCHOOL

We were now living 3 miles from my grandma's house, and my mum and dad had decided that the only option they had was for me to start my education at the infant's school, just a short walk from her house. My grandma was the one who looked after me while my parents were at work, so it was obvious to them that my school should be as close as possible to my grandma's home. My first day started much like the rest of my school life, apart from the fact that my mum would take me to my first day. It started at 6.30am when I was woken up and dressed. We had become friends with our neighbours across the road, and if we cut through their garden, it was a short cut across the fields to the bus stop, but it was still a half mile walk, then it was the bus trip to my grandma's house. My mum would then have to take the bus back and make her way to work and clock on at 8 am, but on my first day, my mum took me to school. I can remember it well, my mum was always late, in fact my dad would often say to her, "it won't surprise me if you were late for your own funeral". We walked into the main hall and all I could see were lots of children sitting cross legged on the floor, and like all brave little boys, I started to cry and clung on to my mum's coat, but to no avail. It didn't take me long to settle in and new friends were made.

When the school holidays came around it was decided we should try and have the Butlins holiday that the year before had only lasted a few hours when we got the news my grandad had died.

I can only imagine after a few "are we there yet" we finally arrived at the holiday camp. I do remember the chalet that we stayed in, only because it had bunk beds, each night I would climb the ladder to the top bunk, but each morning I would wake up in the bottom bunk [not quite sure how that happened]. The dining room was in a long building and it had row after row of tables and chairs and we all sat shoulder to shoulder, but the posh bit was, we had waitresses with white pinnies on, they would serve our soup and then our meat and two veg followed by apple pie and custard. This was the height of luxury, a three-course meal was served to you, and you didn't even have to do the washing up afterwards. We had managed about half our holiday, when, this time, a telegram arrived at the holiday camp, it was quite blunt, as telegrams are, it basically just informed us that my maternal grandma had died. So off home we went again. After the last two devastating holidays at Butlins, we never went there again.

Up to the age of 5 there is not a lot that you can truly say are your own memories. The story of my grandad and the man with the funny hat or the one with my grandma and the bus trip to get the puppy, I'm pretty sure are my memories, but of course most of the last few pages are of stories passed onto me by my parents, either of things that happened before I was born or in the first few years of my life. Now at the end of my infant school years the memories start to become mine.

After my maternal grandma died, I was left with no one to look after me before and after school while my parents were at work. Fortunately, the lady who lived next door to my maternal grandparents said she would help. It was agreed that my parents would pay 15 shillings a week to Mrs Steele, apart from her husband and her brother Jim, who lived with them, no one called her by her first name, it was always Mrs Steele, but I only have the fondest memories of my time with her. My mum still had the job of getting me to Mrs Steele's house before school and collecting me after work, but at the age of seven I was trusted to travel on the bus myself, my mum still took me to the bus stop, then gave me 3d for my bus fare, and that would cover there and back.

I think the 15 shillings was money well spent, I had toast before school done on the open fire. I hated school dinners, so at lunch time she gave me a hot meal and after school, two thick slices of bread, butter, and jam, what more could I ask for?

The junior school was the next stop in my education, and was just a short walk down the High Street, next to the church where my parents were married.

It's at this school that it started to become clear to my parents and the teachers that I wasn't going to be the most academically talented student, but it was early days and hope springs eternal. As for me, I was enjoying my school life, making new friends, and generally having a good time in and outside of school. After the school bell went, I would make my way back to Mrs Steele's house, collect my jam butty, and straight out onto the play park. It was a vast area with swings, slides, a roundabout and many more things to keep us entertained. Our gang of 7 lads would play football, usually with an old leather ball that had seen better days, and our school blazers were the goal posts. Cricket was also a favourite, with 3 pieces of wood knocked into the ground as wickets, a flat piece of wood for the bat and a cricket ball that one of the lads had "conveniently borrowed" from school. The aliens would also use the playpark, skipping and hopscotch was their favoured games. There was one alien who spent time with me, she was my first 'girl' friend, at 7 years old, if she was happy to play football and cricket, instead of skipping that was fine with us. She only lived four doors from Mrs Steele's house, so we spent a lot of time together. Her parents were no different to ours, just ordinary working-class people, but they sent her to a school outside the village, and her uniform was so much smarter than ours, so, we could never use her school blazer as goalposts.

Back at the junior school it was time for the 11+ exam. The school took this exam without me, I was off ill, on my return two days later my teacher asked me to follow her, and I found myself in the school hall with a table and chair sitting in the middle of the room, so this is how I sat my 11+, on my own. I failed, if my parents were disappointed then they didn't show it, but maybe it came as no surprise, as for me, I didn't really care one way or another.

This photograph was taken in my last year in the infant school, it was in the same hall that I arrived late for my first day at school, and they had to prise me from my mum's coat tails to start my education.

The back of this photo says, 'Melvyn, as a tree'. I'm the tree on the left, my lifelong friend Bryn, is third from the left back row, he was the one born at home in the story from page 7, and we still see each other most weeks.

This photo is of my grandma on the left with Mrs Steele. If you look closely, you can see me on the floor looking up at them. You can also see the Anderson shelter [top left] a reminder of the recent WW2 conflict. It was now used to house a few chickens for their eggs. Along with a mate a few years later this would be my first business venture.

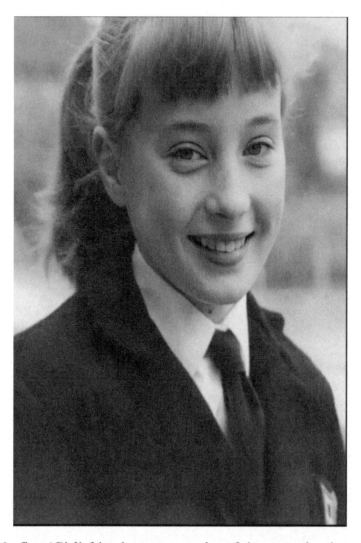

My first 'Girl' friend, we spent a lot of time together in our pre-school and school years. Even though we could never use her school blazer as goalposts, she was, and still is, a very special friend at a very special time of our young lives.

This photo is of the playpark that was at the back of my Grandparents' home and Mrs Steele's house, we were so lucky to have this on our doorstep. My gang of 7 plus my girl-friend and the aliens spent many happy hours here. Mrs Steele's house is the last house on the left of this photo.

Although this photo was taken in the 1970s it's exactly as it was in the 1950s/60s apart from we didn't have the protective cage at the top of the slide, this was H&S edging its way into our life. One thing we did to make the big slide faster, was, to get some waxed paper, we would just sit on the paper and slide down, after a few goes with the waxed paper the slide became much faster.

THE MOST ICONIC
TIME OF MY LIFE

I was 11 years old, and I had stayed up later than normal, but after just two hours in bed, I woke up to singing in the street outside my bedroom window. As I looked out of the window, I could see our next-door neighbours dancing in the road and one of them shouted "IT'S 1960". I wasn't sure what all the fuss was about, and I suppose the next morning nothing had changed, but I wouldn't have to wait long before, Everything Changed!

After school I would spend a couple of hours with my mates then get the bus home. There were times when I would have spent my bus money on sweets, so I had two options, the first was, walk the 3 miles home, and that was fine, but if it was raining, I would resort to plan B, and that was to get on the bus and make my way to the top deck, as I knew the conductor would always go to the people on the lower deck first to collect their fare. Once I was on the top deck, I would look on the floor for a discarded ticket and then sit looking through the window making sure my reclaimed ticket was visible in my hands. When the conductor eventually came to the top deck to collect the fares, he would either see me twiddling with my ticket and think I had already paid, or he would ask to see my ticket, if it was the latter, I would be ejected off the bus at the next stop. By this time, I would have been half way home, not perfect, but better than walking all the way.

On Saturday mornings, we would normally go to the cinema, it was the children's matinee. Our cinema was affectionally known as the flea pit, [not sure why] We would normally go to see a cowboy film, or Flash Gordon, but this Saturday, my mate said the film was Blue Hawaii, starring a bloke called Elvis Presley. There was always a lot of noise inside the cinema coming mainly from the boys, booing at the on-screen villain, and cheering the hero. But on this Saturday the boys were well outnumbered by the Aliens, and the noises they made were more oohs and ahhs as Elvis embraced, kissed, and sang to his onscreen sweetheart. I came out of the cinema that morning not one bit impressed with the film, but the songs that Elvis performed were so different to what we had been used to. Up until this point, all we had was Uncle Mac on the radio, he seemed to play the same thing every week, things like The Three Billy Goats Gruff, or Max Bygraves, singing, "You're a pink toothbrush I'm a blue toothbrush," and, along with many thousands of other kids of my age, we were well and truly fed up with the offerings from the BBC.

This was our local cinema; it was the first cinema to be built in our city of Stoke on Trent, I suppose you could call it Art Deco style. It opened in 1909, but in the early 1960s it was our favourite place to go. On Saturday mornings, it was the kid's matinee, then in the mid-60s I could be found sitting on the back row kissing and holding hands. Also, in 1964 it gave me the chance to see my pop idles on the big screen for the first time.

WHO NEEDS A BUS?

There was a time when if I wanted to get from A to B my only option was to walk, I would never dream of asking my dad if he could take me in his car. At 11 years old I could see that some of my mates were starting to get push bikes, and I wondered how I could get one of these wonderful machines.

Asking for money from my parents to get a bike wasn't something that would have crossed my mind. There were just two occasions in the year when I would be asked what I would like, and that was, Birthdays and Christmas, and it was nowhere near either of those dates. So, I decided I would have to work for it. I started by helping the paper boy to do his evening deliveries. He would pull out the paper from his bag, hand it to me and I would run up the path to the front door, rolling the paper as I went, so that it was the right size for the letter box, then back down for the next one, and on it went. I did this, 5 nights a week for the next 5 weeks, I was paid 6d a week for my labour, and I also got 6d a week pocket money. So now, with my five shillings, I went a few doors down the road to a lad who would build up bikes from spare parts. I handed over my five shillings, and walked away with a bike frame that had two wheels fixed to it, I say I walked away, because I couldn't ride this wonderful machine yet, so I proudly pushed my bike home.

There was a long straight road at the back of our estate that was only used in the daytime, to deliver clay to the brickworks, so I took my bike up there and started to teach myself how to ride. It only took 3 days [with the odd graze on my knees and hands] before I could ride the length of the road without falling off. Can you imagine how I felt with this new found freedom? I could now bike anywhere I wanted to.

I went on the odd bike trip with my mates, I think the furthest we'd gone was to Manifold Valley, a beautiful part of the country that would become a favourite destination with my parents for our annual two weeks' summer holiday, [yes, they now had the luxury of a two-week summer break]

One day my mate Bryn, suggested we should go on a trip to a place called Llangollen. Well, I had visited this place with my parents, it was somewhere they would stop off for an hour or so if we were going to Barmouth or some other holiday destination in Wales. I hadn't a clue how far it was but my dad said that it was not something we could do in a day. He gave me a very old tattered map, and to be honest looking at this map was like trying to read a foreign language, but we drew a line on the map from home to Llangollen.

We set off at about 6 o'clock Friday night, we had everything on our back, a tent, blankets, and tins of beans, also I think we had a few shillings between the two of us. At about nine o'clock we decided to look for somewhere to put up our tent for the night, and looking at the line on our map, we had got just over half way.

We spotted a nice area of grass just over a little wooden bridge, so we put up our tent and opened a tin of beans [cold] we had also got some water and a pack of biscuits. It was about 7-30 the next morning when a man stuck his head into our tent, and by the look on his face, we could tell he wasn't about to wish us good morning. As teenagers back in the 60s we didn't really do a lot of swearing, so, this man taught us a few new words, as apparently, our tent was pitched on part of his garden. Cornflakes were my chosen breakfast back then, and I had put some in a bag, but had forgotten to take milk and a spoon, but that didn't really matter as the head in our tent wasn't going to give us time for breakfast.

We set out on the second part of our trip. It was a very hot day and with our bikes not having any gears, it was proving to be a challenge, and to make matters worse the heat was starting to melt the tarmac on the roads, so we had to keep stopping to scrape the tar off our tyres. We eventually arrived in Llangollen about dinner time. Just over the bridge there was a small café on the right. I can't remember what we had, but it was better than cold beans and water. We asked if there was a camp site, and the café owner told us to go back over the bridge. There was a road opposite and if we just followed this road to the top, it would take us to the camp site. Well, this was one very steep road, it seemed to go on and on. Eventually we reached the camp site, it was just a field on a slope with a few tents on it. We put up our tent and even though we did think of going back down to the town, the thought of biking back up that road, soon put that thought to bed. We did light a fire, and oh the luxury of hot baked beans in our billycans, mopped up with some bread we had got from a shop in town, and we even had a cup of tea. I have got to say it was disgusting, black tea and no sugar. We could make out what looked like the remnants of an old Castle further up the road, normally we would have gone to have a look, but we were knackered, so sleep seemed to be the best option. The next morning, we packed up our tent and went down to Llangollen, the joy of sitting on our bikes and freewheeling to the bottom of that road was the best feeling. We went back to the little café for a slap-up breakfast of toast and jam and a proper cup of tea. We left our bikes outside the café and went a walk around the town and then along the river. At about 2o'clock we decided it was time to make our way home. As we went over the bridge to start our journey back, I could see a car that looked very much like my dad's. I can still remember the registration, it was GVT 156. My mum and dad had decided to have a run out and come to see if we had made it to Llangollen. As the car got closer, I could see two girls in the back seat, they were our next-door neighbours' daughters and, to this day, I have no idea why they were there, apart from the fact that they had just come for the run out. The good thing was that my dad put our camping gear in his boot, so we just had our bikes with no back packs to carry. We made it home about 7pm. I have since found out that it was 50 miles from home to Llangollen. Doing that trip with the types of bikes we have today wouldn't be too much of a task, but the bikes we had then in the 1960s were very heavy and had no gears.

In 2021 my mate suggested we should do a little nostalgic trip to retrace our bike ride 58 years earlier, but this time, along with our wives, we did the trip in style and went by car. I was amazed to find the café just over the bridge was still going.

This photo was taken around the time of the bike ride to Llangollen, I'm the one showing my legs. Over 60 years on, all in this photo are still in regular contact with each other My mate Bryn, who made the bike trip with me isn't in this photo, but we also still meet up most weeks.

MY LAST 4 YEARS AT SCHOOL

I moved from the junior school, to the secondary modern school, which was just a few yards back up the high street. I had my fingers crossed that the first day in my new school wasn't going to be like the first day at the junior school, where the new boys were given an initiation test. We were put up against a wall and a heavy iron gate was swung towards us, if you kept completely still the gate would stop inches from you. It was quite a terrifying experience. Thankfully nothing like that happened at my new school.

It was the first time I had to wear a school uniform, a blazer bearing the school badge, with a piece of coloured felt material that had to be sewn on behind the badge itself, which identified the house team you were in. After assembly, all new pupils were told to go to the notice board in the hallway and look for our name, and above your name would be the class you would be in. It was quite straight forward. The A class was for the clever ones, the B class was for the not quite as clever ones, then there was my class, considering my abject failure of the 11+ exam I suppose I shouldn't have been too surprised, but hope springs eternal.

Being in the C class, had its benefits. The A Class seemed to go home each night ladened down with homework. I don't remember the B Class being handicapped with too much homework, but my Class were free to enjoy ourselves the minute the bell went at 4 o'clock. That's not to say I didn't enjoy some of the lessons. Woodwork [that would come in handy one day]

39

Geography and History could grab my attention, technical drawing was up there as one of my favourite subjects, unfortunately the teacher in technical drawing, was, to put it bluntly, crap. He was an old man nearing retirement, we had tech drawing lessons on Tuesday and Thursday, they were always the first lesson after our lunch break. Clean hands were a must for this lesson, so before I went into the classroom, I would go to the cloakroom, which was just a few feet away, and wash my hands. The first thing this teacher would do was have all the boys stand in a line and inspect our hands. Often, mostly the boys, including me, would get the cane for having dirty hands. If I had known the word sadistic back then, it would have fit this horrible little man. It got so bad that even though I liked the subject, I would skip school after lunch on those days.

Unless I had a good excuse the following morning, I would end up in the Head-master's office and get the cane for skipping school, but in a way, I didn't mind that, as at least it was for something that I had done wrong. One day, before one of those technical drawing lessons, I went into his class room in the lunch break, and went to the cupboard where he kept the cane. I took it out and started to bend it in two, in an attempt to break it. 'WILLIAMS', my name rang out around the empty class room. I looked up to see one of the other teachers standing in the doorway, again, 'WILLIAMS', what do you think you are doing? Well, I thought it was pretty obvious, but I didn't like to say as much, so, I got the cane a bit earlier than normal that day.

In my second year I was deemed to have improved enough to see my name on the notice board under the B class section. It was part way through this second year that the headmaster made an announcement to us all in the morning assembly. He started off by telling us that it was with great sadness that he had to inform us that Mr #####, had passed away. This was the teacher who loved to cane me for supposedly having dirty hands when only 5 minutes before I had washed them. So, forgive me if I didn't share the headmaster's great sadness that day.

Now, we had a new teacher for our technical drawing lessons, his name was John Sandywell. He was a tall, stocky man, and you knew not to mess with him. He was strict but fair. I found him to be a good teacher, so one of my favourite subjects was back on track. I even had some of my work put on display around the school, that was a really good feeling, and gave me a lot more confidence.

My English teacher had all but given up on me, but he was obliged to keep trying. One day he announced that for homework, [Homework !!! even though I had now progressed to the B class, homework wasn't a word we would hear very often] he was asking us to write a thesis on any subject of our choice. After a large intake of breath at the thought of homework, my next thought was, what the bloody hell is a thesis?

I went home and told my mum of this unwelcome extra activity. 'Oh', was her only comment. When my dad got home from work my mum mentioned the homework to him. I could see a blank look on his face, so that made three of us who didn't know what a thesis was! A few weeks earlier my dad, had, in an attempt, to improve my education, taken up an offer from a door-to-door salesman to buy a set of 12 encyclopaedias on a monthly payment plan. Finding out what the word thesis meant became homework in itself, not only for me, but for my mum and dad as well. Eventually, after searching through the encyclopaedias, I had it explained to me. Now all I had to do was work out what could be the topic for my homework. After a lot of thought I decided on Ants, so I went to the encyclopaedias again for help. There was quite a long

41

section on Ants, and I found these little insects fascinating. I would never have believed how strong and organised they were. They worked as a team, something we could all learn from. So, I set about writing my thesis. At first, I started to copy sections from the book just to get me started, after a while, I could see the book explained it much better than I could. So, it seemed obvious to me that if [1] I copied what was in the book the teacher would get a better understanding of my thesis, [2] the homework would be finished much quicker, and [3] I could get back outside with my mates. The following week I handed in my homework, the next day the teacher called me to his desk to tell me how impressed he was, and not only that, he said it was the best by far in the class.

At the end of term prize giving awards, I was called to the stage, and given a book token as a reward for my thesis. How they didn't work out it was copied word for word from the encyclopaedia I will never know, but as they say, never look a gift horse etc. Also, if they could cane me for no reason then why not get a prize for simply copying from a book ☺

1963 IT ALL STARTED HERE

Suddenly, I had gone from scruffy school boy to a dedicated follower of fashion, also, the aliens started to look different to us lads.

There was talk amongst my friends about this radio program that was on late at night, it was called Radio Luxembourg, and you had to tune into 208 medium-wave to listen. We had a radio that took pride of place in the corner of our living room which my parents would listen to most nights, but my dad had just bought a portable radio to take with us on our camping holidays. So, I took this radio to my bedroom and started to turn the dial to 208. It crackled, it faded in and out, but the music was like nothing I'd heard before. One of my first memories from this radio station wasn't even a song, it was an instrumental called Telstar by a group called The Tornados, but this was just the start.

In early 1963, I came across a BBC radio program called Brian Matthews Saturday Club. I thought the music was a big improvement to what the Beeb had normally been turning out. Then, he played a song called Misery, by a group called The Beatles, although it's not a song that many people, in years to come, would call a classic Beatles song, but at that time, I thought it was one of the best songs I'd heard. Walking to school the following Monday, I saw two of my mates talking to two girls, [by now we were showing more interest in the aliens] when I got up to them, they were looking at a postcard size photo of 4 men and they all looked the same, they had the same haircut and were wearing the same jackets. I asked who they were, and one of the girls said, it's The Beatles, as soon as she said the name, I remembered it was the same name that I had heard on the Brian Matthews program, and she went on to say that they were trying to work out who was who in the photo. I'm not sure how I managed it, but I walked away, with that photo tucked in my pocket. When I got home, I got 4 drawing pins and I pinned the photo to the curtain pelmet that went across the top of the living room window, it took my mum about two hours before she spotted it. 'I don't know who they are', she said, 'but you can take it down. This became the first of many Beatles' photos to be put up on my bedroom wall.

It was quite a few years later that I found out the song, Misery, was written by Lennon and McCartney backstage before their performance at the King's Hall Stoke-on-Trent on the 26th January 1963, just 4 miles from my home. They were virtually unknown at this time, apart from the teenagers in Liverpool, and a dedicated group of teenagers, who visited the night clubs in Hamburg, West Germany, where, their then manager, Alan Williams, had sent them in 1960. It was playing up to 8 hours a night in the Hamburg nightclubs and the Cavern club in Liverpool that The Beatles perfected their stage act.

It took them just 10 months from their Appearance, as virtual unknowns, at the Kings Hall, Stoke, in January 1963, to topping the bill at the Royal Variety show in London. At the time, this was the biggest televised show of the year, they performed just 4 songs that night. Their last song was called Twist and Shout, John Lennon [that's him, bottom right, in the photo on the next page] stood looking out at the audience, and with a twinkle in his eye, he said, 'for our last number I'd like your help, for those in the cheaper seats, clap your hands, and then looking up at the Royal Box', he said, 'and the rest of you just rattle your jewellery'. It was their wit, sense of humour and musical talent that set them above many other groups that were springing up all over the country in 1963, but that's not to say the other new groups weren't producing some of the classic songs from that time.

From early 1963 to the end of that year the pop charts had gone from the old crooners of the 1950s and very early 60s to an explosion of pop music. Some were from America, but the majority were from all corners of the UK. As teenagers, we could hardly keep up with the fantastic songs that were coming over the airwaves, and even television, were jumping on the band wagon. On Friday 9th August 1963 we had *Ready Steady Go!* Their catchphrase was, "The Weekend Starts Here." So, we could now see the groups, and individual singers, albeit, in black and white. [no one had colour telly back then]

This is the first photo of The Beatles, that I managed to get from one of the girls from school. I hadn't worked out who was who yet.

Ready Steady Go, was a must watch for teenagers, but the presenter, a man named, Keith Fordyce, looked more like your dad rather than someone more suited to present a show aimed at thirteen- to sixteen-year-old kids, but they did get one thing right. Keith's co-presenter was a young trendy girl named Cathy McGowan, most of us boys fancied her, and a lot of the girls would copy her hair style, and her clothes were the height of fashion.

After The Beatles had performed at the *Royal Variety Show,* the Daily Mirror [the largest selling newspaper at the time] front page headline, was, *"BEATLEMANIA!" Is Born,* this was a reference to all the teenage girls who would squeal, non-stop, from the second their name was mentioned. This trend would soon catch on, and most groups, who were in the music charts, [the top 20] would get a similar reaction from the girls. It got so bad that no one could hear the groups on stage, the decibels the girls were making with their screaming was likened to a jet aircraft taking off, in fact the groups themselves said they couldn't hear their own guitars or drums.

In 1964, the music kept on coming, if anything, there was more of it, and the songs were definitely getting better. We now had BBC1, BBC2, and ITV, they were all playing catchup, to provide the increasing demand from teenagers for more pop music programs. *Ready Steady Go* was now joined by *Thank Your Lucky Stars,* and *Juke Box Jury,* the latter was a programme where 4 pop stars of the day would sit behind a table and each would have two cards one would have **HIT** and the other would have **MISS** written on them. The compere, David Jacobs, would press a button, and a record from a juke box would lower onto the turntable and play a few seconds of a new pop song, and the 4 celebrity guests would decide whether they thought it would be a **HIT** or a **MISS** in the top twenty pop charts. As you can imagine, it wasn't the most exciting pop music program, but we all watched it just to get a glimpse of our pop heroes. Although, there was a sting in the tail, every now and then, after the celebrities had voted, they would bring out one of the artists whose record had just been played, and it could get quite embarrassing if the song had been voted a **MISS,** by the panel.

I remember sitting in a small cafe, in our town one Saturday morning with my mum. It was 1964, and someone had left the Daily Mirror newspaper on our table, the front-page headline in bold print said, **LIVERPOOL V TOTTENHAM.** This would be something that you would normally expect to see on the back of the newspaper with all the sports news. Even though I wasn't too interested in football at that time, in the small print under the headline, I spotted a name that I was interested in. It said, who would win the battle for the top spot in the pop charts, The Beatles, or The Dave Clark 5. The headline was a reference to The Beatles, who came from Liverpool and The Dave Clark 5 who came from Tottenham. At the time The Beatles were number 1# with "I Want to Hold Your Hand", and the Dave Clark 5 had just released a song called "Glad All Over". The following day the new pop charts were printed in the Sunday paper, and Glad All Over had knocked The Beatles off the top spot. Now, 58 years on from that headline, I'm now, interested in football, and my local team, Port Vale, always play the Dave Clark 5 song, Glad All Over, when we score a goal, and all the supporters join in singing along to it. In 1964 there were many critics of the new pop music, mainly from the older generation, who said, 'this new *noise,* that they try to call music, will never last, give it 12 months, and it will all be forgotten', *how wrong they were.*

There were two more programmes that were a must for teenagers in 1964, one was on the television and the other on the radio. The television programme was called *Top of the Pops,* and was on Thursday nights. This was the best chance we had to see our pop heroes perform their latest songs. The studio was set out like a night club, with a stage and a few dozen teenagers on the dance floor. It was on programmes like this that we were able to see our pop heroes, and started to copy their hair styles and clothes. Pre-1963 the worst thing my mum could say to me was: "I'm taking you to get new shoes or some new clothes", but now I was begging her for Cuban heel boots and a collarless jacket like The Beatles wore! Also, a must, was the high-necked shirts, like The Dave Clark 5 were wearing. These shirts went really well with the collarless jacket. A visit to the hairdresser's [well we didn't call them hairdressers back then, it was the Barber's] was a must, but we had to grow our hair long first, then walk into the Barber's shop and ask for a ***Beatle cut***. The radio program that was a must listen was the Top 20 on Sunday night, it started at number 20 and moved up through the charts until the grand finale revealed the number 1# that week. The most famous presenter was Alan Freeman, he made the show a national institution, and would start by saying ***Hi Their Pop Pickers.*** All the above are just examples of how, in just 12 months, the Radio, Television and even the Newspapers were desperately trying to keep up with the speed that pop music was moving at and the demand for more, via *Teenagers,* who were now spending money on clothes and records.

In 1964 I was on holiday with my parents, and we were walking along the seafront, when I spotted a huge banner over the front of the local Cinema, it announced, **THE BEATLES,** in their first full length movie, ***A HARD***

**DAY'S NIGHT.** I pointed at the banner, and asked my parents if we could go to see it. "Not now son", was my dad's reply. I gave it my best shot to change his mind, but no amount of pleading worked. My mum tried to calm me down, by saying, 'when we get home, I'm sure it will be on at our local Cinema.' ☹ This wasn't what I wanted to hear, but I didn't have much option, other than to hope, my mum was right.

Back home, and, as normal, mums are usually right! The film was on at our local cinema, so, along with three of my mates, off we went. Now, I had seen the girls screaming on the pop programs on the telly, but inside that cinema the screaming was on a different level. Every time they caught a glimpse of one of the Beatles they started screaming, and, as the film was all about the Beatles, and they were on the screen most of the time, the screaming was non-stop. I was sitting next to one of the girls, and before the film started, we got talking to each other. I thought she was very attractive and maybe this was my lucky day. Then the film started, and it soon became obvious that her favourite was _Paul McCartney,_ and, suddenly, she had gone from the nice girl I'd been talking to, to jumping up and down, shouting hysterically, '**Paul**, I love you, will you marry me!'. It soon became obvious that I had just been a stop gap until the main event. The only contact I had with her after the film had started, was me helping her up off the floor after she had tried to stand on her seat and had fallen off!

All these girls screaming got me thinking, so, on our way home, I said to my three mates that we should form a group which they all seemed up for. The fact we couldn't play guitars or drums or hadn't got any money to get these magical instruments didn't stop us dreaming.

49

It was now time to find out who was the best singer and who would do backing vocals. A few weeks earlier one of my mates had had this little machine that was no bigger than a cigarette packet, which he told us could record anything we wanted. We were all fascinated by this. he pressed a button and told us to say something, and, like magic, we could hear back what we had just said. I couldn't get over it, none of us had seen anything like it before. Now, on the day of our singing audition, we all sat in the house of the lad who had this little tape recorder. We were each to choose one of the popular songs of the day to sing as our audition. No one wanted to go first as we were all a bit shy, so, my mate with the tape recorder, had an idea. He suggested that if we took the recorder into the kitchen on our own, and recorded our chosen song, then it could be played back and a vote would be taken to discover who was the best singer. When it was my turn, I took the tape recorder into the kitchen, pressed record, and started my audition. I finished my song, pressed stop, and opened the door, only to see all three of my mates rolling round laughing. Apparently, they had been listening through the door and it became obvious, without even a vote, that I wouldn't be the lead singer, in fact I wasn't even a contender for backing vocals ☹.

I mentioned to my mum, my failure to pass the singing audition, she told me not to worry as it was probably because my voice was breaking 😯.

I remembered about 12 months earlier when I was standing in our living room singing along to a Cliff Richard song on the radio, I think it was Summer Holiday. When my duet with Cliff had finished, I asked my mum if she thought I sounded like Cliff. Now, I don't know if she wasn't feeling very mumsy at the time, but without a second thought, she said, 'no son, you don't'. So, now, I was left wondering how long it was going to take for my voice to break! It wasn't long after my failed singing audition, and the obvious lack of musical instruments, that our band decided to call it a day before we had even started.

We decided, instead, that it was time to start concentrating on improving our images. The 2-inch Cuban heel boots, I'd seen in a shop in town were 19 shillings and 6 pence or 19/6d. The best chance I had of getting these was to ask my mum for the money. In fact, everything I wanted, as far as clothes were concerned, was best run by my mum first. The request for the boots was easily resolved. I was given a £1 note and wasn't even asked to give mum the 6d change. The collarless jacket was a bit more of a challenge. A discussion took place between my parents. My dad couldn't understand why I would want a jacket without a collar, but a shrug of his shoulders and walking off shaking his head was as close to a 'Yes' as I was going to get, so that was two down! Now, for the high collared shirt, like The Dave Clark 5 wore. This time my dad was a bit more vocal, 'bloody hell', he said, 'first he wants a jacket without a collar, now he wants a shirt with a massive collar!' He walked away, not only shaking his head, but muttering something under his breath, but I could cope with a bit of muttering. That was three down! Now, to finish off my new look I just needed a pair of trousers with a wide belt. Fortunately, this didn't even need a discussion, but my mum said she would go with me to choose them. The leg bottoms had to be eleven and a half inches, 'you're not having them that tight', she said, 'you will never get them over your feet'. 'I will', I said. 'No, you won't!' So, it was 13" leg bottoms I ended up with, which was totally unacceptable, but I had a plan.

Mrs Steele, the lady who had looked after me from the age of 5 all through my school years, had a sewing machine and altered clothes for people to earn a bit of pin money. So, on Monday morning, I sat warming my knees by the fire while Mrs Steele altered my 13" leg bottoms down to eleven and a half inches. When I got home, I could see my mum keep looking at me, but she couldn't work out what was different. Mrs Steele was always on my side, so I didn't have to worry about her saying anything to my mum.

My hair style at the time was the traditional short back and sides with a very neat parting and Brylcreem kept it all in place. This look had become an image breaker. I was normally given 2 shillings, once every 3 or 4 weeks to go to the barbers, [hairdressers] to get my hair cut, but now, letting my hair grow much longer wasn't something that would go unnoticed. The day arrived and I was given 2/- [2 shillings] to go to the Barbers after school to have my hair cut. Mrs Steele's sewing equipment came to the rescue again. By now I had stopped using Brylcreem, so my usually combed back hair, was now combed forward into a fringe. All I needed to do was to use Mrs Steel's dress making scissors to trim my fringe, which is what I did, and no one was the wiser. After about three lots of 2 shillings, my dad said, 'I thought you were supposed to get your hair cut?' 'I have done', I said. Well, it wasn't a lie, because he didn't ask who had cut it.

It was only after the next 2/- that further questions were asked. This time my dad said, 'I thought you were getting your hair cut today?' 'I did', was my reply. 'Where did you go?' Now it was my turn to mutter under my breath. 'Right', he said 'let's go'. 'Go, go where, I said, 'You will see'. We got in the car, to be honest, I felt quite privileged because I was sitting in the front seat. We made the 3mile trip to the Barbers shop near to my school. When we walked through the door, my dad said, 'Bill, what do you call this?' pointing at my hair. Bill said, 'I don't know, what do you call it? A bloody mess, is what it is," my dad said. 'Well,' Bill said, long hair is the fashion now. 'So, you think this is alright, do you?' my dad asked. 'It has got nothing to do with me', said Bill, 'I haven't seen him in weeks!'. So, I was unceremoniously put in the Barber's chair, and all my hard work was undone in a matter of minutes by Bill's shears. We didn't speak on the way home, but when I got in, I said to my mum, 'he doesn't know what fashion is', making sure my dad could hear. 'I'm going to look a right idiot at school tomorrow'. The next day my mum said, 'me and your dad have been talking, and we don't mind you having your hair a bit longer, so long as you go the Barbers and get it done properly'. To be honest, I thought I was doing a good job of it myself.

A bit of a spinoff to come out of my unwelcome visit to the Barbers, was, as Bill was butchering my hair, he was talking to my dad about a part time business he had, and which he was thinking of selling. It was, apparently, on the allotment just across the road from my school.

I remember hearing my mum and dad talking a few weeks earlier when my dad said that he wouldn't mind getting a little part time job to earn some extra money. So, now talking to Bill the Barber, it was agreed that my dad would take a look at this business venture and a meeting was arranged with Bill on the allotment. I was roped in to going to this meeting with my mum and dad. I'm not sure what contribution I could have made to this meeting as I was only 13, but if it was anything like any of the other ideas my dad had had, it would normally involve my mum and me as labourers.

When we moved into our council flat, my dad decided to build a garage for his car. There was a site about a quarter of a mile away that the council set aside for people to put their garages on for a small land rent. My dad decided to build his garage in the back garden first, but make it a sectional one, so that when it was finished it could be dismantled and taken to its permanent site on the council land. It was about 20ft x 10ft and made with a timber frame and corrugated sheets. My dad wasn't known for his sense of humour, but if you can imagine our back garden was only accessed by a narrow path that went between the flats to one side and the brick coalhouse on the other side, there was no chance of getting access for a car. The lady in the flat below us, who we shared the garden with, never really got involved in the garden. She was happy to let my dad do what he wanted with it, but curiosity must have got the better of her, and she asked, how my dad was going to get his car into the garage, my dad told her that he was going to build a ramp over the brick coalhouse to the back, she just said, 'Oh, I was wondering how you would do it □

When the garage was finished my dad got 3 of our neighbours, along with my mum and me, to carry each section of the garage at a time over the quarter of a mile to its new, permanent home. I was also recruited to help him dig a 4ft deep pit in the garage floor so he could do any maintenance underneath the car. I can't tell you how many hours I spent standing in that garage, passing tools to my dad, who would be down that pit doing whatever was needed, I hated that garage with a passion.

Back at the allotment, we met up with Bill, and stood outside a building that was about 50ft long and 20ft wide, with a big cobbled area to one side and an 8ft square building stuck on the end of the main building. Bill said that the small building was the boiler house, and, sitting on

54

the cobbled area, was a very battered old van that had the roof cut off. When Bill opened the door to the main building, it was pitch black inside, with shutters up to what few windows there were. I could just see row after row of shelves, that stood about six-feet high, with wooden boxes on them and as soon as we walked inside, the heat hit you. Bill's little business turned out to be a mushroom growing business, from which all the local shops would buy their mushrooms from, also, the allotment people would buy an odd punnet or two. This was the only time I visited this building until the day came that I was told my dad had bought it.

At the weekend all three of us went to the allotment. My dad had been given a list of all the local stables and the three of us sat in the old van that had the roof cut off. We set out to call at all the stables on the list. At every one we visited we were shown to a big pile of horse manure that had been cleared out of the stables, and it soon became clear why the van had its roof cut off. We all had our own pitchfork and set about loading all this manure into the back of the van through the roof, it didn't take long for my dad to put his pitchfork down and wander off to talk to the owner of the stables. I was never told what these conversations were about, but it normally lasted until mum and me had put all the horse manure into the back of the van! After visiting about three stables the van was full, so it was back to the allotment to unload our smelly load. The back doors of the van were opened and we emptied it out on to the cobbled area. Then, back on the road to visit more stables, this went on until we had the biggest pile of horse manure you could imagine. After about 4 days we had to move the pile of horse manure, putting the outside to the inside so the heat generated by the manure would help to break it down. As this process was taking place, the next

55

job was to visit fishmongers and anyone who had wooden boxes that could be used to grow the mushrooms in. I thought the horse manure was smelly, but that was nothing compared to the smell from the fishmonger's boxes. All the boxes had to be dipped into a tank of disinfectant. Bails of peat were delivered along with some other magical ingredients, all this was mixed with the horse manure, then all the boxes we had collected, of which there were 120, had to be filled and carried inside, placed onto the rows of shelving, 10 boxes in each row and three rows high. The final stage was to plant the mushroom spores, job done, well, that's what I thought.

The boiler house with the coke fire had to be kept lit 24/7 and all the boxes had to have a water mist sprayed over them 3 times a day. So now, I had to set out for school an hour earlier, to top up the coke fire that provided the central heating in the building, and then, go inside the building and spray the water over all the boxes. My dad had said that the door to the building must be kept closed, to keep the heat in. We didn't have any electricity on the allotment, so, I can tell you, as a 13year old, it was the most frightening thing, to be inside this building in the pitch black, walking up and down these 6ft high rows, spraying each box. I had to repeat it all again after school, it didn't take me long to recruit the help of one of my mates, just to keep me company in this dark damp dungeon of a building. My dad's contribution was to call on his way home from work.

After a few weeks the mushrooms started to spring to life, I was spared the picking, weighing, boxing up, and finally delivering them to all the local shops. When the mushrooms had finally given their best, it was time to empty all the spent mushroom compost from the 120 boxes. We took them outside and tipped them onto the cobbled area, it was quite a sight to behold. All the gardeners who had an allotment, were like bees round a honey pot, they all arrived with their wheel barrows. They were filling them up and almost running to their individual plots, emptying the contents, then back to refill them. The compost from the 120 boxes was cleared up within an hour. Apparently, this spent mushroom compost was Gold Standard as far as growing almost anything on the allotment, something, my dad was quick to realise could become another money maker.

With my twice daily visits to the allotment, I got to know many of the gardeners. One of them had a greenhouse, and he said that his tomatoes were the best, and gave me one to sample. I'm no expert, but it tasted very nice. I asked if they were grown in the mushroom compost. 'No, it's a very special compost', he said, tapping the side of his nose with his forefinger. As a 13year old I hadn't got a clue what this gesture meant. He then ushered me out of the greenhouse and lifted up a tarpaulin sheet, looking over his shoulder to make sure no one was looking. 'It's this, he said, what is it?' I asked. 'It's human excrement', he said. 'Human what?', I asked. 'Shit, human shit!'. It would be many years before I could eat a tomato after that. Just a few years later this magical tomato grower, became my best mate's father-in-law.

It was after about 12 months of mushroom growing that my dad announced that we wouldn't be growing mushrooms any more. He said, it was a lot of hard work for little profit, phew, I thought, thank goodness for that. I can't ever remember being paid a penny for my labours, so this was good news.

My good news, however, was short lived. Apparently, my dad had found an American company who grew mushrooms on a massive scale. They were based in

Derbyshire and they used some underground tunnels that had been abandoned after the war to grow their mushrooms in. They had a big problem with the mountains of the spent mushroom compost that they struggled to get rid of. My dad found out that if anyone wanted any of this spent compost, all they had to do was turn up with a wagon, and they would load it up with no charge as they were just happy to get rid of it. A very large high sided coal wagon was hired for the day and my dad along with the driver set off for Derbyshire and returned with 10 tons of compost. The compost was tipped onto the cobbled area and a note was put up in the hut that was used by all the gardeners for their committee meetings which were a very serious affair. Allotment rules were strict and a person could be brought before the committee if they were found guilty of breaking any rules. Apparently, the note my dad put up in the shed informed all gardeners that this pile of compost was not to be used for general distribution around the allotment. It must have been torture for the gardeners to see all this Gold Standard compost just sitting there, and they were being denied even a barrow full. Now instead of visiting stables we went to the local farmers who had mountains of empty fertilizer bags that were ideal for putting our spent mushroom compost in. The idea was to advertise in the local paper, 4 bags for a £1 delivered. My mum would hold the bag and I would fill them, my dad would do his normal and wander off talking to anyone who would listen.

The local advertising proved very popular, and we were soon struggling to keep up with the orders, so my dad had a brilliant idea, he made two stands that would hold the bags, so now we could fill twice as many. I was never sure why he didn't make three stands, but I suppose there were many important conversations to be had. After the first load, my dad was called in front of the Allotment committee, he was told that Allotments were for growing produce and not for storing compost. A compromise was reached. After each load was delivered the gardeners on the Allotment were aloud 2 barrows of the compost free. My dad did very well out of this little business and soon made enough money to buy a new car from the profits, me and my mum were very happy for him.

CHRISTMAS IN THE 1950s/60s

It seems strange sitting in my garden, in the shade, and it's still 28 degrees, writing my memories of Christmas in the 50s and 60s. Many of the pop stars who were aiming to get a Christmas number one, in the pop charts, would very often have to plan ahead. They recorded their song, in the height of summer, and the recording studio would be decked out to look like Christmas, just to get them in the right frame of mind. I didn't fancy getting the Christmas decorations out to give me inspiration, but, if I had, I am sure that someone in my family would have called for the men in white coats to come and take me away.

For an 8 year old, Christmas was probably the most exciting time of the year. I think we had two mail-order catalogues in our house, Kay's and Grattan's to choose from. I would sit for hours going through the toy sections. The problem was that I was told to choose one thing for my main present, it was torturous trying to make a decision. Eventually, I pointed to my chosen toy, my mum said, 'we will put it on your list, and hope that Santa thinks you've been a good boy'. The rest of my list included things like, the Dandy and Beano annuals, a selection box, the obligatory orange and nuts, although you had to work hard for your nuts. You would place them into a nut cracker and squeeze the handles together, there was definately a technique. If you squeezed too hard the shell would fly across the room and you would squash your nuts! ☹ One year I had a kaleidoscope, which was a cardboard cylinder you put your eye up to the small hole, and turned the cylinder to see coloured shapes making different patterns, this held my attention for about 10 minutes. My main present the same year was a walkie talkie, one end of which had a button you pressed that gave off a buzzing sound at the other end, to alert whoever you wanted to talk to. This wasn't remote controlled, it had a long cable from one hand set to the other. I would sit in my bedroom and press the buzzer, more often than not it would be my mum who answered it, but after a day of this, she had an idea. Our neighbours, in the next flat, had a son who was about two years older than me, so it was decided that, as we both lived on the top floor, if I leaned out of our living room window and he leaned out of his, we could swing the hand set to and fro until he caught it, then we could talk to each other. I thought that talking to someone in the next flat was a brilliant idea. At first it was great, my mum was talking to his mum, even my dad found it fascinating and joined in. At this time, no one had telephones, so to be able to talk to your neighbours from your own livingroom was quite an experience. After the first day, I kept pressing the buzzer, but got no reply, I opened the window to see if the cable had got damaged. Instead of the cable going into their living room window, it was swinging below ours, with the hand set still connected, apparently they had got so fed up of me constantly pressing the buzzer they had chucked it out of the window! So now it was back in my bedroom and my mum had the privilege, once again, of answering my calls. She did pop her head around my bedroom door and said, in a stern voice, 'please stop pressing that buzzer'. A few days later the walkie talkie went missing. I never did find out what happened to it.

My dad loved Christmas, but it was mainly my mum who made the most effort with the decorations. The first Christmas tree that I can remember looked like a broom stick with bottle brushes sticking out, all sprayed green for that magical look. The decorations were mostly home made, but we did have a set of 12 lights that looked like lanterns. The radio was moved from its table at the far corner of the living room to make way for the tree. Christmas cards were put across the pelmet over the window or pinned to the wall. My parents didn't really drink alcohol, apart from the odd drink if they were out with friends, or at Christmas, when they would have a small selection to offer visitors.

Saturday morning was the day we would all go into our local town. I would be dragged around the shops, and, knowing there wouldn't be much in it for me, it wasn't something I looked forward to, but there was one shop that definately got my attention. This shop was right at the top of the Town square, it was a big double fronted shop, and just looking through the window excited me. Every toy you could dream of was inside this shop. The main attraction this particular year was the huge train set they had set out. Normally, I would count myself lucky just to stand outside looking through the window, but as Christmas got near, my dad would take me inside this magical shop while my mum carried on doing whatever food shopping they had come to do.

Once inside the shop, I pointed to a little steam engine called Nellie, no big fuss was made by my dad regarding my excitement over this steam engine, and as it was November I thought there was little to no chance of me having it. Back outside my dream shop, we met up with my mum and made our way to another shop just across the square. This shop held absolutely no interest for me, the shelves were stacked with all sorts of different bottles of beer, wine and spirits. My parents visited this shop most Saturdays, but never seemed to buy anything. My mum would get out a card and hand over half a crown (2/6d) and the lady behind the counter would make a mark on the card then give it back to my mum. Apparently, this was a savings card and when it got close to Christmas, whatever they had paid onto the card could be used to buy alcohol for Christmas. The drinks I can remember were, a bottle of Teachers whiskey for my dad. This bottle had a different shaped cap to any others, and was used as a measure for the whiskey. Dad also had a soda syphon which was a very ornate glass bottle with a lever on the top and a spout; press the lever and the soda water, under pressure, shot out of the spout. My mum chose Babycham and Advocaat and there would also be a bottle of Port and a bottle of Sherry. I can never remember them buying any beer, but on one occasion my dad did attempt to brew his own beer! There were big Demijohn bottles used for fermenting his beer and the biggest saucepan was used to bring all his ingredients to the boil, and simmer for hours on the cooker. The smell was horrible and stunk the whole flat out, then, when the special thermometer told him it was time, he put it into bottles. They were stored in the airing cupboard for what seemed weeks. We were watching the telly one night, when loud noises came from the airing cupboard, 4 of his 12 bottles had decided they had had enough and popped their corks, the mess and smell in the airing cupboard didn't impress my mum.

My mum in the living room of our flat, Christmas 1961.We had moved on from the artificial Christmas tree, and gone upmarket to a real one.

I wonder how many of you remember your first Christmas tree looking like the one pictured above?

Tower square Tunstall, in the 1960s. My favourite toy shop was at the top on the left, and the shop my parents paid 2/6d a week to, on a savings card, for their Christmas drinks, was on the right.

Our little Town was a wonderful shopping centre in the 1960s. We had two cinemas, the posh one, and the one that most kids went to for the Saturday morning matinee, affectionately known as the flea pit. The high street had every sort of shop you could wish for, Boots chemist, Woolworths, Banks, Burton's clothes shop, and above Burtons were two snooker rooms. We also had a wonderful park, with a boating lake, band stand, two football pitches, tennis courts, and a bowling green. It's only looking back now, that I realise how fortunate we were. Tunstall today, 2022, along with most of our towns, looks more like a third world country. The high street now is full of boarded-up shops, with the odd take-a-way, charity shops and food banks.

I came home from playing with my mates one day, to find a table about the size of my bed sitting in my bedroom. This table wasn't like something you would find in the window of a furniture shop, it just had 4 legs and a frame with a hardboard top. I asked my mum what it was for, she just said, 'your dad is making a table', not exactly an answer. I now had just about room to walk between my bed and this table. As I spent very little time in there, it didn't bother me too much. My dad was always making something, so I didn't give it much thought.

Christmas Eve, we all got in the car and set off to visit our relatives. First on the list was my dad's brother. He was a happy man, and always made a fuss of me. They had 3 children and lived in a very small terraced house. No presents were ever exchanged. My mum would have a cup of tea, my dad would have a small whiskey. I can't remember ever being asked if I wanted a drink. From there we moved on to my mum's sister. They lived in what I thought was a very posh house. It was a three-bedroomed semi-detached, with beautiful views from the back and it wasn't owned by the council or rented, very unusual, for the 1950s/60s. They had taken a mortgage to buy it. Occasionally, I would sleep over at my mum's sister's house and she would look after me if my parents were out for the night. My mum and her sister worked together on the Pot Banks. One of their jobs was sticking handles on cups and, who knows, whether the cup you are drinking out of, had the handle stuck on to it by my mum or her sister. My mum's brother-in-law was a Desert Rat in World War Two. He never talked about his war times and was a very modest man. The next on our visiting list, was my mum's brother, who lived literally across the road from my mum's sister. Looking at old photos, he was a carbon copy of my maternal grandad. I always thought that my uncle's wife was a dedicated, follower of fashion. She had a blonde bouffant hairstyle and wore a twin set, also her make-up was a bit over the top. I say that, because my mum wore very little make up, so, my aunty reminded me of the ladies you saw in magazines. Even though, my dad didn't drink much, I would imagine that by the time we got home, he had probably had a bit more to drink than he should have had. In his defence, the law wasn't as strict as it is today, and I can never remember either my mum or dad being drunk.

By the time we got back home, it was bed time for me. The excitement was building for the big day, I thought, if I pretended that I was asleep, maybe, I would catch a glimpse of the Main Man, but sleep won.

Normally, my mum had a job to get me out of bed, but the next morning, I was out of bed and made my way to the living room. As I opened the living room door, it all looked different. It was dark and the usual welcoming coal fire, that I would sit by with my cornflakes and cup of tea, was just a black hole. I went to my parent's bedroom. 'It's only 5 o'clock, go back to bed', was the groggy voice from my dad. I went back to my room huffing and puffing and climbed back into bed. It was my mum who, at about 8 o'clock, woke me up. It became a standing joke in future Christmases, when I asked my dad if he had set his alarm for 5 o'clock.

As I walked into the living room, I could see lots of little parcels wrapped up on the table by the tree. As I started to open them, it soon became obvious, what the table in my bedroom was for. The last parcel, that had been kept back from me, was Nellie, the steam engine that I had got excited about in my favourite toy shop. It took, what seemed forever, to set it all together on the table in my bedroom. I think my dad was as excited as I was with my train set, in fact, after Christmas, he was the one to suggest we visit my favourite toy shop, and add the odd station box and bridge to what was now, OUR train set. Nellie the steam engine was probably my best Christmas present, up to now.

Nellie, my favourite steam engine

In the early 1960s, as a teenager, there was no looking through catalogues or visiting toy shops for inspiration for my main Christmas present. Along with many teenagers there was only one thing I wanted. The black disc that we called a 45 needed a record player to play it on. The most popular record player was called the Dansette. Hinting at what I wanted for Christmas was too much of a risk. There were two shops in town that sold them, and even though, by now, I had stopped going shopping with my parents on

Saturdays, 'after all, teenage boys didn't do things like that', but one Saturday before Christmas, I had to make an exception. As we got to one of the electrical shops that had a Dansette record player proudly displayed in the window, I made it clear that this was the one. Along with the record player, I was hoping for perhaps one or two records, or even better, an LP to play on it.

Christmas morning, like most families in our City, breakfast, along with bacon, eggs, cheese and tomatoes, we had the Staffordshire Oatcakes, and they were a must. For anyone who is not familiar with them, they are the shape and thickness of a thin pancake, but made from oatmeal, strong flour and yeast, sounds simple, but we had, and still have, many Oatcake shops, who guard their recipes like the crown jewels. If you ever get the chance to try one of our local delicacies, start with a warm Oatcake, put on melted Cheshire cheese and cooked tomatoes, topped off with crispy bacon, then roll your Oatcake and cut it in half before dipping it into a soft egg. They are delicious beyond belief. A word of warning, Oatcakes sold from supermarkets are not of the same quality as those bought from a traditional Oatcake shop □. Christmas lunch, was roast chicken [what a treat that was] with all the trimmings. My mum was first class at overcooking most things, but I never realised this until I left home. Christmas lunch had to be done and dusted before 3 o'clock, so that we could sit and watch the Queens Speech. Christmas tea, was tinned fruit, evaporated milk with bread and butter, to be fair, we probably also had ham or tinned salmon and cucumber sandwiches.

As I write this, I am saddened to say, we have just had the devastating news, that our beloved Queen Elizabeth II, has passed away, I can't express my sadness, she was a beacon of light in our lives. GOD BLESS THE QUEEN.

Christmas morning, in the 1960s, as a teenager, there was no longer a 5am start to my Christmas day. My mum came to wake me up at 8 o'clock. When I walked into the living room, I could see one of my wrapped presents that looked the size of a Dansette record player. When I picked it up, I couldn't believe how heavy it was. I ripped off the paper, and the picture on the box looked nothing like a record player, when I lifted the lid, I could see two round disks, but it was not what I was expecting. I think my mum could see the puzzled look on my face, then my dad said, 'this is better than a record player'.' What is it?' I asked, 'it's a tape recorder', he said, quickly followed by, 'it's the best one you can get'. He then went into detail as to why it was better than a record player. 'First, he said, you can record all your favourite songs from the radio, so you don't have to buy them.' He then said 'each tape will hold the equivalent of 30 records.' He could see by the look on my face that I wasn't convinced, so he went on to tell me that each record costs 6/9d so think how much that will save me. Now it was my turn, 'what about LPs?' I asked. 'Well,' he said, 'you can buy any LP, on tape', and proudly gave me another present. It was an LP that I had asked for, but it was on tape. I've got to admit this did bring a smile to my face. 'What about singles, how do I record them?' 'Well, you can record them from the radio', he said smugly, 'but how do I know when the radio will play the song I want to record? Do I have to sit by the radio with my finger on the record button and hope they say what they are about to play?'. He had a glazed look in his eyes, I could tell he hadn't thought of that one!

71

My little eureka moment came when I was looking in the Sunday papers. They printed the Top Twenty songs in the charts and on Sunday night the BBC would play the Top Twenty on the radio, so with the information from the Sunday paper, I could plan what songs I wanted to record, and, at what number it was in the charts. If a friend had an LP that I wanted, I would just take my tape recorder to their house and record it. There were now television programs, like, Top of the Pops that I could also record. One big problem with this was that I could be recording from the radio or television, and my dad would ask for a cup of tea or my mum would decide to use the vacuum cleaner or the dog would start barking, and all these sounds would feature on my recordings. One of my favourite recordings was The Beatles performance at the Royal Variety Show. I still have the tape recorder, and that recording, along with all the other songs from that time, although, now, my most treasured recordings are the ones with my parent's interruptions. My dad asking for a cup of tea, my mum putting the vacuum cleaner on, or Lassy barking. These were the sounds that so annoyed me back then, when I was trying to record a song from the radio or TV, but now, 60 years on, they are far more important to me than any of the songs I was trying to record. I think it's safe to say, my dad got this present right.

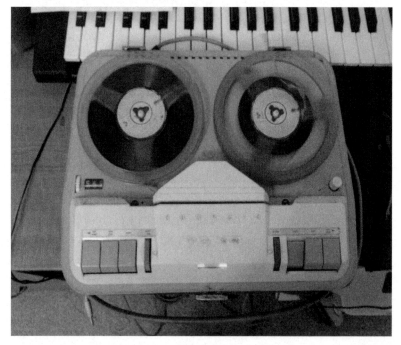

The top picture is two of the LPs that I had on tape. They were about a quarter of the size of the vinyl LPs, but sounded and looked identical, and they all had the same information on the back. The picture below them is the tape recorder that my dad insisted was better than a record player. It's a Grundig TK 14 and is now 60 years old. It not only works perfectly, but also all the recordings that I made, including, The Beatles at The Royal Variety Performance in 1963. They all sound just as good as on the day I recorded them. It's amazing how I remember so many of the recordings and can picture in my mind when I recorded them, but I struggle to remember what I did yesterday.

HOW THE SHOPS
CAME TO US

Living on a big council estate, over a mile from the town centre, could be a problem regarding fresh food. We had a pantry with a cold slab that meat and similar foods would be placed on to help keep them fresh, but without a refrigerator, some food shopping had to be done almost daily. I'm not sure who designed our estate, but with over 300 houses and flats on it, the designers would have done a better job if they had just taken the time to asked for the advice of any housewife. All these homes, and not one shop.

Thankfully, there were small businesses who spotted the opportunity to bring their shop to all these customers. Nowadays, you may hear the ice cream van making its way around the streets. Back in the 50s and 60s our ice cream man was named Peter, the chimes of Greensleeves could be heard many streets away, which gave you the time to quickly run in and say, 'Peters coming, can I have an ice cream, PLEASE', sometimes it would be 'No, you had one yesterday' but, if you were lucky, 4d would be put in your hand, and you ran back out and stood by the curb. Peter's ice cream was the best. He was a tall happy man and with his special scoop, he would lean into his freezer and scoop out this yellow gold, and with a squeeze on the handle your cornet was handed to you, for an extra 2d you could have a chocolate flake added, better known as a 99.

The ice cream van was just one of many businesses that would drive around our streets. We had two fruit and veg vans that came. One of these was driven by a man who would pull up, get out, and stand by his van, and with a voice that any Town Crier would be proud of, left you in no doubt he was there. The other one had a big flat backed truck with a canopy to protect the veg from any rain. This seemed to be a family business, with a man, his wife and young son and they announced their arrival with three long blasts on the horn. They also sold sweets and chocolate, my favourite was a small box that had chocolate covered nuts and raisins, again, I had to beg for a few pennies if I had any chance of getting my hands on one of these boxes.

Like everyone back then, we had the milk man, the bread man, the paper boy, and we also had the van that delivered Pop. The coal man would have a note left, instructing him how many bags you wanted and it was always a good idea to have more than needed during the summer, so you could build up a stock ready for winter. With no central heating, we also had a van that came round selling paraffin. He would fill up your own can from a tank in the back of his van. Even though we now had an indoor toilet and bathroom, the paraffin heater was a must in winter. The smell from the paraffin heater wasn't the best in the world, but it was nice to walk into a warm bathroom in winter. There was also a van that came round selling fish. I don't ever remember us having any fish, probably because my mum wasn't sure what to do with it.

You may remember I mentioned that with our Christmas breakfast, it was a must to have the Staffordshire Oatcakes, well Oatcakes were not just for Christmas. Most Sundays, we would have them with our breakfast, so the Oatcake van was always very popular. So, you can see, even though we didn't have any shops on our estate, the shops came to us.

Entrepreneur, is said to be a person taking financial risks in the hope of making a profit, but was never part of my vocabulary, especially when I first dipped my toe into a business venture. When I was 10 years old, along with a mate, we were in the local shop next to my school, probably buying 1d chews or something similar, when a man came into the shop with a tray of eggs. He handed them to Mrs Beech, the shopkeeper, she opened her till and handed him some money. When we left the shop, I said to my mate, 'we could do that!'! 'Do what', he asked, 'sell eggs', I said.

One of my relatives had an allotment, so I asked him if we could use part of it to keep some chickens on. At first, he said no, but I kept on at him until he gave in. He did say we would have to fence it off and build a hut to keep the chickens in. My building skills were limited at 10 years old, but with some help from my allotment relative, we had something that resembled a fenced off area, and a hut that was a bit like a big dog kennel. We went to a local farm and asked if we could have 6 hens. The farmer said he had some pullets we could have, and he wanted 10 shillings, 'Pullets? We want hens.' After he explained that pullets were young hens, I went and asked for 5 shillings from my dad, with the promise, that I would pay it back when we sold our first eggs. My mate did the same. We proudly put our pullets into a box and carried them to the allotment. Every day before and after school we went and fed corn to them. That was another problem, we had to spend time collecting old pop bottles, and taking them to the shop who gave us 1d for each bottle. We also collected scrap iron, and took it to the scrap yard to earn a few more pennies. This was how we got the money to buy the corn.

Each day we looked for eggs, this went on for weeks, with nothing. We never saw an egg. I suppose it must have had something to do with not realising that a cockerel was an important part of the plan, or we were just impatient. I honestly can't remember what happened to the chickens, but my first business venture didn't work out as planned.

77

One thing we found out by keeping the chickens however, was, we could make some money from collecting scrap metal, and taking it to the scrap yard. One bright idea we had was, after the scrap yard had closed, we climbed over the fence, and lowered ourselves down inside the scrap yard thinking that, if, we threw a bit of scrap back over the fencing, then we could take it back the next day for a few more pennies. I think this sort of thing must have happened before, because just as we got inside the scrap yard, we heard this growling and barking. When we both looked around, all we could see was this very angry Alsatian dog running towards us. We just managed to get back over the fence, with the dog snapping at our heels. I'm often reminded of that night, when I see a sign on someone's garden gate, with the picture of a dog, WARNING, I can make the gate in 3 seconds, CAN YOU?

I was lucky enough to visit Pompeii a few years ago, and I had to smile, when I saw at the entrance to one of the Villas, a Mosaique of a big dog, it was obviously a warning, 'enter at your peril' so, even the Romans in 79 A.D had worked out that, just the thought of a dog roaming free inside, would help to protect their property.

The mosaic of the guard dog at the entrance to one of the Villas in Pompeii

The next venture to make some money wasn't so much a business plan, but an opportunity. Walking the streets [we did a lot of that back then] with another mate, [see, I had more than one mate] we came across a big roll of wire wrapped around a wooden cable reel, we couldn't help ourselves. We started to roll it down the road and onto the fields. This is not my proudest moment, but we decided to set fire to the cable so that we could take the wire to the scrap yard. One thing we didn't realise was the amount of smoke that would come off the casing around the wire. There was so much black smoke going up into the air that we got scared and ran off, we thought that someone would ring the fire brigade. The next day we went back to the scene of our crime, only to find our plan had worked, there was a big pile of tangled copper wire. We dragged it across the fields to the scrap yard, and instead of the normal pennies that we were used to getting, he got out his wallet and gave us £2. We thought we were rich, and I suppose we were, considering my pocket money was 6d a week.

Just to try and redecm myself from the last two stories, and to show that I could be a good boy, occasionally. I remember walking home from school one lunch time, when I spotted a piece of coloured paper in some long grass at the side of the pavement. When I picked it up, I realised it was a ten-shilling note. I took it to Mrs Steele, [the lady who looked after me through my school years] who thought we should take it to the police station in the village. The policeman told us, that if it wasn't claimed within 3 months, it would be returned to us. After about a week, a lady came and knocked on Mrs Steele's door. Apparently, she had reported to the police, that she had lost the ten-shilling note. She was so pleased to get her money back that she came to say thank you and gave me 2/- [two shillings] as a reward.

It's hard to belive that in the 1950s, the 10 shilling note, could have such value that it seemed right to take it to the police station, and put it into their lost property. Today its equivalent is the 50p coin, I don't think many of us would lose any sleep if we lost 50p. In the 1950s your 10 shillings could quite easily be enough to take you to the cinema, call in at the pub for a pint or two, pick up a chippie supper and get the bus home, and you would still have change from your 10 shillings.

I recently found the following on a social media site, it relates to other people's memories of finding a 10 shilling note in the 1950s. Below you will see some of the quotes made by people who found a 10 shilling note, and how much it ment to them.

Loved the 10 Bob note , found one once when I was 8 thought I was really rich 😄

18 h   Like   Reply   7 👍

Yes I found one too at about the same age. I wouldn't steal it! Handed it in at the Post Office. It wasn't claimed after 3 months and so they gave it to me.

18 h   Like   Reply   1 👍

yes I handed mine into the police station , same thing for me .

17 h   Like   Reply   1 👍

snap! Found a 10 shilling note in the street, handed into police station. 3 months later got it back and shared with my brother. Thought I was really rich . I was about 9 years old!

My Entrepreneur skills definitely required some fine tuning, but I wasn't going to be put off. Over my lifetime, I would, try, try and try again.

81

HOLIDAYS OVER THE YEARS

GOOD, BAD AND SAD

As you may remember, our two holidays at Butlins, when I was 4 and 5 years old, had sad memories. The first was, when we arrived at the holiday camp, and a phone call to the camp, informed us that my maternal granddad had died. The second time, we had been there for a few days, when we had a telegram informing us that my maternal grandma had died. So, understandably, the following year, a Butlins holiday was not on the list.

As a youngster, my dad would go camping at a place called Manifold Valley in the Peak District, this would have been in the 1930s. So, after our last two disastrous holidays, he decided to buy a tent, and off we set for a week's holiday camping underneath the stars. I would imagine that he chose Manifold Valley because of his own childhood memories. This was definitely the first holiday that I can remember, and it was wonderful.

We set up our tent on a small camp site in the valley, right next to the river Manifold. The only problem was, the river was nowhere to be seen. There was a very wide and rocky river bed, but without any flowing water, and at my young age, I never gave it a thought to ask why a river didn't have any water. All I knew was, it was the place my dad would build a camp fire, and we would sit on the rocks in the river bed at night time, drinking tea, with the water being boiled on the camp fire, and the best jacket potatoes you could ever wish for. On the opposite side of the dry river bed was a steep slope with lots of trees. I followed my dad into the wooded area, as apparently we were looking

82

for some very special branches. After about an hour of searching, we returned to our camp site with two long branches and two shorter ones, the short ones were definitely the hardest to find, they had to be straight and thin. My dad got his knife out and started to carve the long branches, at this point I lost interest, and talked my mum into playing football with me. I don't think she was too keen on the idea, but after a few minutes there were some other kids on the camp site that just joined in. It took me a while to notice that my mum had made her way back to our tent. It's only recently, thinking back on those camping holidays, that I realised what hard work it must have been for my mum. Breakfast, Lunch and Dinner all had to be prepared on a Primus stove. One thing that did save time, was that we had just bought a new kitchen appliance called a pressure cooker, so all the vegetables could be done in one go, and kept warm while she cooked the chops or whatever else we would be having. I can only remember us lighting a fire at night time, so the primus stove was all she had. After this first camping trip, a second primus stove was invested in, I bet my mum was pleased ☺.

The farmer, who owned the camp site lived just a short walk away over a wooden bridge that went over the river with no water in it. We went there for our drinking water as he had a tap outside his cow shed. Two 5 gallon drums would keep us going for the day, and my mum also took the washing up bowl from home, so, this was how we had a wash every morning. I can tell you, that water was freezing. The only time we boiled the water was for doing the dishes, making a cup of tea in the daytime or for my dad to have a shave. The farmer also sold eggs, bacon, sausages and milk, they were all his own produce and we had to take our own container for the milk, which came straight from the big milk churn. He would even sell a chicken, which had to be ordered the day before! We never had a chicken.

My dad spent quite a lot of time working on the 4 branches that we had got from the wood. The two long ones now had a piece of string attached to each end and Robin Hood would have been proud of it. It was now time to turn the two smaller branches into arrows, this required a trip over the wooden bridge to the farm yard to search for feathers that the hens had discarded, these were fixed to the arrows and a point put on the opposite end.

Me with my dad trying out our Bow and Arrows

When my dad bought the tent, he went to the Army and Navy shop and bought 3 old army camp beds [you can see them in the photo] they were probably the most uncomfortable beds you could imagine, just a hard piece of canvas stretched over a wooden frame. He also made the folding chairs himself, and a three-sided piece of aluminium which became a shield that went around the primus stove to stop the wind from blowing it out. You can also see our new kitchen appliance, the pressure cooker which made it so much easier when cooking on just one primus stove. The camp site was just 15 miles from home. A few years after my first camping holiday, when I was 13, I suggested to 3 of my mates, that we could go camping there. It was during the Easter school holidays. The plan was to go on our push bikes, but my dad had just bought a Bedford van to deliver his mushroom compost, and he offered to take us. So, with all our camping gear and us 4 lads in the back of the van we set off. If my mum and dad's camping gear looked basic, it was quite luxurious compared to what we took with us. A very small tent, no camp beds, and no primus stove, but we did have our billy cans and a kettle. The idea was to cook our meals on the camp fire in the dry river bed. The first morning we woke up to snow, but as young lads this didn't bother us. We spent the day exploring, then we lit a fire, to cook our beans and jacket potatoes. Before we went to our tent for the night, we decided to build up the fire and put our wet coats around it to dry. The next morning it sounded like someone had left a tap running, I poked my head out of the tent, it wasn't raining, but as I looked towards, what had always been a dry river bed, all I could see was a fast- flowing river. It took a few minutes, before I remembered we had left our coats around the camp fire.

We saw the farmer walking along the bank side, it looked like he was searching for something. He told us he was looking for any sheep that may have been washed down the river, and if we saw anything, to let him know. He said the river would spend months underground, then without warning it would just reappear. I mentioned we had left our coats around the fire the night before, and they had been washed away, he pointed to the bridge just a few yards away, and told us that there was a wire mesh fence across the river under the bridge, which was to stop any sheep being carried down the river, and suggested we look there. He was right, so, it was shoes and socks off and trousers rolled up, as we waded in the river to rescue our coats. Perhaps Easter wasn't the best time to go camping!

Our next holiday was much further away, it was at Cheddar Gorge, but it was still a camping holiday. This time, because I'm an only child, my mum and dad decided that I needed a holiday buddy. They chose the girl who lived opposite us, she was 12 months older than me.

I didn't have any say in it, but we were mates, so I didn't mind. The idea was, the two of us were going to share a small tent, [we were very innocent back then]. We arrived at our camp site, and I remember we were in the Valley, and looking up at the Gorge, it was very impressive. The primus stove was unpacked, and we had a cup of tea, then we went a walk along the Valley. Not long into our walk, I spotted a sign saying, beware of snakes, I thought this was worth a question, my dad just said, 'they are Adders', Adders'!!! I said, 'what are they?' 'Well, they are a venomous snake', 'venomous, what's that', 'well if they bite you, it could make you poorly'. Now, there was no way I would be sleeping in a tent with these snakes roaming round. So, Elaine and I spent the holiday sleeping in the car. My mum and dad tried to say it was nothing to worry about, but they couldn't kid us, we had seen the sign! I slept in the well of the car, between the front and back seat, and Elaine slept on the back seat. As far as I can remember it was a good holiday, with a good mate to keep me company. We never saw a snake that holiday, but I put that down to our astute preventive actions. Although on a subsequent holiday, I let my guard down.

Me on the right with my mate, Bryn, on the camp site that in 1963 we went camping on and lost our coats when the river decided to reappear. This photo was taken in 2021, just a mere 58 years on from our camping trip. My mate suggested this nostalgic trip and, along with our wives, we had a brilliant day

Top picture me with Elaine, my holiday buddy, you can see the front of our snake-safe sleeping accommodation in the background. I didn't find out until years later that Elaine was adopted, her mum and dad were wonderful people. I spent many happy hours helping her dad in his garden [well I think I was helping] I remember I was in their house when Wagon Train was first shown on the TV, do you remember that program with Ward Bond. The bottom photo, with my dad, at a place called Wookey Hole Caves.

Over the next few years my holiday buddy would be someone different each year. I can't ever remember being asked who I would like to keep me company. Sometimes, I wouldn't know until the day of our holiday, who would be the chosen one.

One of the strangest choices was the son of a man who worked with my dad, who was dropped off at our house on the morning of our holiday, and this was the first time I had met him. They lived about 8 miles from our home, so even if we hit it off on the holiday, the chances of him becoming a long-term mate were slim. The older I got, the more annoyed I became at not being asked who I would like to take. We had moved on from camping holidays to renting a caravan for two weeks and had booked a holiday in Barmouth. This year my cousin, on my dad's side was chosen, he was two years older than me. We weren't mates, but my dad would instigate little competitive games between the two of us, things like, see who was the fastest runner, or the best at arm wrestling. With him being two years older than me often he would win almost everything. One of the challenging games, that was suggested by my dad, was, to see who could run to the top of a steep hill that was at the back of the caravan site. Ready Steady Go, and off we went up the hill, half way up, there was a dry-stone wall that we had to climb over, and, at this point, we were neck and neck. I jumped up and grabbed the top of the wall and, as I pulled myself up, I came face to face with a snake that was curled up on the top, if anyone had got a stop watch, I'm sure I would have set some sort of record running back down that hill. I had spent one holiday sleeping in the car to avoid snakes, so this little encounter just confirmed we had made the right decision.

The following year, my dad decided that my cousin should be my holiday buddy again. This time I put my foot down,

I said that I wouldn't go on holiday with them if that was the case. I would rather stay with Mrs Steele, than go through that again. There were a lot of raised voices, but eventually, I was, at last, asked, who I wanted to go on holiday with me. My answer was obviously my best mate, after some discussion with my mate's parents, at last, I had someone who I wanted to share my holiday with.

I ended up having three holidays with my best mate keeping me company, Barmouth, Great Yarmouth, and finally, in 1966, Cornwall. This would be the last holiday that I would spend with my parents. From now on, I would go it alone, well, not alone, but with other people.

You may remember, I previously said I wasn't interested in football, in fact, in 1966, on this Cornish holiday, my mate and I were walking along a cliff top track trying to find a way down to the beach below. After about an hour or so we gave up, and headed back. It just so happened that at the same time as our cliff top walk, England were playing West Germany in the iconic World Cup Final. We had moved on from camping and caravan holidays, now, for this holiday in Cornwall, my parents had rented a bungalow [how posh were we]. When we got back from our cliff top walk, my dad informed us that England had won the World Cup. We just shrugged our shoulders at this news, we hadn't even realised that they were playing, but over the next few weeks, my interest in football would change.

Me on the right, with my mate Bryn, on my final holiday with my parents.

LEAVING SCHOOL ON FRIDAY

STARTING WORK ON MONDAY

In my last week at school, we were told to go to the main hall. There were chairs placed along the back wall, and in the middle of the hall there was a table with a man sitting at it. He wasn't a teacher or anyone that I had seen before. When your name was called, we had to go and sit at the table with this stranger.

Question by the man, 'what do you want to do for a job?'

Me, 'pardon'.

Man, 'what do you want to do for work, when you leave school?'

Me, 'I don't know'.

Man, 'well, what are you good at in school?'

Me, thinking very hard to find an answer to this question, eventually said, 'Technical Drawing, and Woodwork'.

Man, 'you can go back to your class room now'.

Two days later, and my final day at school, we were told to go to the hall again. This time, the man at the table was a different man, but the same procedure. He called my name and I went and sat at the table. He looked at his notes, and said, 'so, you want to be a joiner?'

Me, 'what's a joiner?'

Man, 'you said you were good at woodwork?'

Me, 'yes'.

He again, looks at his notes, and then, writing on a card, the name and address of a building firm, he gives me the card, and tells me to go to this building firm's office after school. No other instructions were given, apart from, 'you can go back to your class now'.

At four o'clock the school bell rings for the final time and I walk out of the gates. I recognised the name on the card which the man had given me, and told me to call in to see them after school. I walked past this building on my way home which was an old chapel that had closed, and the building firm was using it as their workshop. Next to it was a new extension which they used for their office. So, with my little card in hand, I went through the door. All I could see was a wall with a frosted glass hatch. I knocked on the hatch, nothing, so, I knocked again. Eventually it slid open, and a little man, whose head was just about visible above the counter top, said, quite abruptly, 'YES', so I handed him my card. He closed the hatch and after about 5 minutes it opened again and the little man just said, 'come to the yard at 7.30am on Monday', and shut the hatch door again. I went home in a daze! I hadn't got a clue what was going on. When my mum and dad arrived home from work, I explained what had happened, they both seemed very pleased and my mum said, 'well done'. I thought, what are you talking about. Apparently, I had just got myself a job as an apprentice joiner. When I walked out of the school gates, I naively thought that I would at least have my normal 6 weeks holiday first.

On the Monday morning I was dragged out of bed at 6 o'clock. I sat in front of our newly fitted posh gas fire and my mum put a cup of tea and a bowl of cornflakes in my hand. 'Hurry up, you don't want to be late' she said as my empty cup and bowl were taken from me. I was given a small canvas bag with a tin mug, tea leaves scrunched up in paper, milk in an old camp coffee jar, two rounds of jam and two rounds of ham and sent out into the world of work.

I remember saying to my mum. Have I got to do this now for the next 50 years? Apparently, I had. ☹

I made my way across the fields at the back of our estate, it was a short cut to the builder's yard. As I went around the corner of the building, I could see a wagon with its engine running and a canopy perched on the back. Two men were standing by the wagon, smoking, and talking, and another group of about 6 men standing together. They all looked quite scruffy, one of them even had a cowboy hat and boots on. No one took any notice of me, so I stood with my back to the wall looking down at the ground. After a few minutes a man in a suit came round the corner, apparently, he was the site manager. He went and spoke to the wagon driver, then he gave a quick nod to the other men, then it was my turn. He asked my name and where I lived, so, I obviously gave my name and address, he said, 'I don't want to know your f***ing address, I just want to know what area you come from'. I was quite nervous to start with, but those few words had made me feel much worse. I was then told to climb on the back of the wagon, and sit under the canopy along with the other men. One of the men sitting next to me told me not to take any notice of him, meaning, the site manager, because he was like that with everyone and no one liked him. We went about 3 miles bouncing about on the back of that wagon before we reached the building site. I was told to put my canvas bag in a big hut, then, I was taken to a partly built house and introduced to a man named Derek, who was to be the one who would pass on his joinery wisdom to me. Thankfully, Derek was a nice mild-mannered man. This was my first day at work in 1964.

Over the next few years as an apprentice joiner, I would have many run-ins with this horrible site manager, but over time, and with growing confidence, I would find subtle ways of getting my own back, and often, encouraged by my work mates, as they wanted to enjoy the pay back.

This is a very old and grainy photo, taken at about the same time as my first day at work story in 1964. The building in the centre of the photo is the old chapel that was now used by the building firm [J.W.Walton Builders] where I started my apprenticeship, and where I stood, as a 15-year-old, with my back to the wall, feeling nervous, and the bully of a site manager, did nothing to help my nerves. In the distance, the long building on the left of the road, with the tall bit sticking up, was the Pot Bank [pottery manufacturers] where my mum worked. I love to include photographs, relevant to the stories. As the saying goes, 'A picture is worth a thousand words!' I feel so lucky that, my mum saved so many photos and other information from that time. I worry, that now-a-days, photos taken on our phones will eventually disappear into the ether, and be gone forever.

95

After my initial shock of being thrust into the world of work, I started to see it had some benefits. One was, that each Friday, I was presented with a little brown envelope containing my wages, £3-3 shillings. I can only remember, that it was agreed, that my parents would have £1-10 shillings and that I would have £1-10 shillings, so the 3 shillings must have been deductions taken by the UK treasury. Just the thought of having this money to myself was exciting, the days of begging for a few pennies from my parents were gone. At the age of 16 I had a dream, it was a bit like the dream I had of owning my own push bike, but this dream was on a different level. I decided that I wanted my own car, and 10 shillings were more than enough to last me the week. So, in a little brown tin under my bed, I started to save a pound a week. Obviously, it didn't work out like this every week, there were times when I wanted to buy the latest Beatles LP for my tape recorder, or some new fashion item, after all I had an image to maintain.

One Saturday, along with a couple of my mates we were walking around our town, and in a shop window, we spotted these bright coloured shirts and corduroy hipster trousers with a wide belt. It was all the different colours of these shirts and trousers that got our attention. We decided they were a must buy. The shirts were in like a shiny silk material and the trousers a heavy cord. We each decided to have different colours, my choice was orange trousers with a purple shirt. Back at home I presented my new look to my parents, my mum just said, "words fail me" and my dad did what he always did, "rolled his eyes, shook his head, and walked off muttering to himself.

Back at work, I now had a canvas bag to carry my ever-increasing tool collection. Each day we would climb on the back of the wagon that would be waiting outside the workshop and take us to whichever site we were working on. I had been on quite a few different sites in my first 12 months. Occasionally, the horrible site manager, who had managed to make me a nervous wreck on my first day, would walk around the site with the foreman, checking on the progress. I knew that if he came to my section, he would deliberately start to pick fault with whatever I was doing. Normally, it was like water off a duck's back, but every now and then I would stand my ground, and answer back. We could end up in a full-blown row, which usually ended up with him sending me home, and suspending me for a day, without pay. Not the best outcome, as my wages would be down on payday.

Around 18 months into my apprenticeship, I was working on an extension to a school, when the wagon that dropped us off each morning, rolled onto the site. Bill, the driver came to me and said that I had to collect all my tools and go with him. I asked, why and where were we going, he just said that he had been told to take me back to the joiner's workshop. I travelled back in style, sitting in the cab alongside Bill. When we arrived at the workshop, I got my tool bag and went in, not quite knowing what to expect. The joiner's workshop was somewhere that most of us would like to work, it had many plus points, first it was dry and warm, it had a proper toilet with hot and cold running water. On the building sites, in winter you would be freezing cold, and if it was raining you got wet and had to carry on. The toilet was just a 3 feet square hut with a bucket, that some poor labourer would have to empty. The joiner's workshop only had two joiners and two apprentices working in it. They would make all the things that were none standard, it also had all the electrical tools, like planers, mortice machines and ripsaws, these were the sort of things you would have to do by hand on the building site. The foreman was a man named Joe, he was about mid 50's, and wore a bib and brace overall, but always wore a shirt and tie. Joe just told me that the previous apprentice along with his parents had emigrated to Canada, so I was to replace him. I couldn't believe my luck, out of all the apprentices on the sites I was the chosen one. My first job was to make sure the water boiler was full and boiling for lunchtime, so we could make our cup of tea. We all had our own chair to sit on around the fire eating our lunch, it was only then that I noticed a door to the right, that had the word, office on it. A cold shudder went down my spine, this was the office of the horrible site manager. On the sites, I would see him every few weeks, now it would be every day. The first time he walked in, I was working with Brian, the other joiner, he came over to me and asked why I had let the workshop get in such a mess, and told me to get a sweeping brush and clean it up. No big deal, I thought, after all it was a job, an apprentice would do. The next day, it was sending me to collect a box of nails from a supplier at the far end of town, this was about a two-mile walk, and the box of nails weighed about 10 lbs. When I got back, with my arms feeling like they were about to drop off, Joe, the foreman, said that they would normally send a van to collect things like this. These little things started to happen quite often, and it didn't take long for me to realise that Tony, the other apprentice was never asked to do things like this. I got on very well with Joe, Brian, and Tony, they became good teachers, Tony, the other apprentice was about 12 months older than me, but he wasn't one bit interested in music or fashion, he still had a very old-fashioned hair style, he wore a bib and brace overall that was much too big for him, and a pair of glasses that always seemed about to fall off the end of his nose, but we hit it off, and became good friends.

The straw that broke the camel's back, was the day the horrible site manager came and told me that I would have to go to a compound that we had across the road. It was a place that was used for storing sand, gravel, and cement. This day, a delivery of cement needed to be unloaded. When I got there, the driver couldn't believe it was just me that had been sent to unload this cement. Normally, it would be two labourers that would do this job, it was 2 tons of cement, 40 bags, the driver stood on the back of his wagon and lowered the cement bags onto my shoulder, and I carried them into the container. Apart from the weight of the cement, each bag was fresh cement, so it was very hot, my shoulders felt like they were on fire.

It wasn't just me that this bully would pick on, talking to others that I had worked with on the building sites, they would tell me of similar things that he would do or say to make their life difficult. I had stopped arguing back, as this could end up with me losing a day's pay. So, I started to think of ways of paying him back. Each Friday, I was expected to go to the chip shop, and if he was in, his choice was always a steak pie, I thought a little sawdust mixed in with his pie would be a start, it had to be hardwood sawdust so it blended in with the pie filling. I quite simply eased the pie lid up and sprinkled a little inside. I spent my lunch time looking at his office door, wondering if he was enjoying his pie. He did come to me later in the afternoon and asked me if I had been to a different chip shop 😊. One of the jobs that the apprentice would do, was to put primer paint on any doors or windows that we had made. I thought a little blob of this pink paint on his office chair was worth a go. When he eventually came out of his office, I could see a pink splattering of paint on his backside. These little things may seem juvenile and I suppose coming

99

from a 16-year-old, they were, but at the time it was all I could do. Unlike today, there was no one or anywhere I could go, to complain about his bullying. I would take papers, or building plans from his desk and enjoy watching him searching for them, then the next day, I would put them back. One thing I did, that wasn't my idea, it came from an apprentice bricklayer, who was going through similar treatment as me from the bully. He suggested I put something in his car that would smell, his suggestion wasn't something I could bring myself to do, but it gave me an idea. I brought a tin of sardines from home. I discreetly, and, Individually, placed them inside his car, over time, this turned out to be a good one. He even asked the firms mechanic to try and find where the smell was coming from. I only found this out when I overheard the mechanic and Joe the foreman talking about it.

Normally, our days were confined to the workshop, but on one occasion, along with Brian, I was sent to do a job for a friend and neighbour of the Big Boss. It was in a very posh little town, called Alsager, about 4 miles from the workshop. Brian, had his own car, so we travelled in style and arrived at Pikemere road. The houses in this road were like nothing I had seen before, they were big detached houses, and I suppose looking back, they could be described as Georgian style. The job we had to do, was to fit some boards to the wall of their new conservatory. These boards were a new idea, they were 8ft x 4ft plywood sheets but had a design on the front that made them look like rows of individual boards, this design was called, Knotty Pine. As I have mentioned before, working on site back in the 1960s, we didn't have electric tools like drills or saws, everything had to be done by hand. So, to fix these plywood sheets, we first had to fix wooden battens to the wall. Today you would simply use a drill and a masonry bit, then put a rawl plug in to fix too. Back then we had a special tool called a plugging chisel, we had 16 battens and each batten had 4 fixings, so, 64 holes had to be chiselled out. The mortar between the bricks was very hard. Brian marked out all the holes, then gave me the hammer and chisel, after about 20 holes, my right arm was aching, and I had lost count of the number of times I'd hit my knuckles with the hammer. I suggested to Brian, that, perhaps, he should do some, he seemed to think this was below his pay grade, and that it was the apprentice's job.

I understood, that an apprentice was expected to do some menial jobs. In fact, one of my jobs, twice a week, was to go to the office, with a bag, and empty all the waste paper bins. At each room, I would have to knock on the door then wait to be invited in. The first was the boss's secretary, she was very nice, and always asked how I was doing. In the next room, was John, the boss's son, he was about 2 years older than me, and was training to be a quantity surveyor. Even though John came from a well-to-do family, and of course, I didn't, we still had quite a few things in common. We would talk about music, the clothes he wore were right up there with the fashion of the day, and he had the best Beatles haircut. The last room on the top floor to get my bin emptying service was the Big Boss himself, he was a stocky man with grey slicked back hair. I can't say I ever had much of a conversation with him, he would just pick his bin up and pass it to me, but he was always polite and thanked me. Back down stairs the last room was sparse compared to upstairs, it was the office that I went to on the day I called on my way home from school, and got the job. The little man was still there and still just as rude, two other women would be typing away. I did lots of other menial jobs that didn't exactly enhance my apprenticeship, but with Brian insisting it was my job to

101

chisel out all the 64 slots, I felt was unfair. I did another 10 or so, then I said, it's now your turn. He insisted it was my job, so I put down the hammer and chisel, got my coat and walked out. I made my way to the main road, and started to walk the 4 miles back to the workshop, it was wintertime, and not the best time for a walk. I had got about half a mile down the road, when a car pulled up alongside me. The driver wound down the window, and a voice said, don't you work for me? When I looked in the car, I could see it was the Big Boss himself. I just said, yes. Where are you going, he asked, I'm just going back to the workshop, get in, I will give you a lift. I sat in his posh Rover car; it had leather seats and a fancy walnut dashboard. He didn't even ask why I was walking 4 miles back to the workshop, but he did ask where I was working, I said, on the job in Pikemere road, oh, on the conservatory? I just said, yes, and that was his only questions. I was always struck at the smell of his aftershave, whether it was when I was emptying his waste bin, or now sitting in his car, it was overpowering. The men I knew, just didn't smell like this!!

When we got back to the workshop, I just got out of the car, and thanked him for the lift. As I walked into the workshop, Joe, the foreman, obviously wanted to know what was going on. I did my best to explain, he didn't make any comment, he just gave me a menial job to do. The following day, Brian and Joe were in conversation, and this time, it was Tony, the other apprentice who went with Brian, to finish the job. I did ask Tony if he had to finish off chiselling out the slots, he said, no, they were all done. The moral of this story, is, don't let anyone bully you into doing something you shouldn't be doing.

I spent just over 12 months working in the joiner's workshop, even though it was quite a comfortable environment to work in, I didn't feel I was getting the experience that I had when working on the building sites. On the sites, you were never given menial jobs, it was 100% joinery. So, to be sent back out on to the buildings site was perfect for me.

HOW IT HAS CHANGED 1964 to 2022

These two photos are taken from roughly the same spot. The old chapel that was the joiner's workshop has been demolished, and replaced by a convenience store. One thing that is very noticeable in the two photos is, the lack of traffic in the old photo compared to the one taken in 2022. The only thing that has remained the same is the gable end of the house on the left of both photos.

TRANSPORT AND NEW INTERESTS

In 1966 when we got back from our holiday in Cornwall, [that turned out to be my last holiday with my parents] my mum came home from work one day, and started to tell me about a lady that had just started to work with her. She said, that this lady, along with her family, had just moved onto our estate, and that her eldest son, who was about the same age as me, didn't know many people of his age on the estate. She suggested to my mum, that it would be nice if I called at their house, and for want of a better phrase, take him under my wing, and introduce him to some of my mates to help him settle in. My mum told me where he lived, and that I should call round and introduce myself. I couldn't believe what she was asking me to do, I said, you want me to go to some stranger's house, knock on their door, and say, I've come to take your son on a tour of the estate. I was still only 16, and that's not something a 16year old lad would do. After a lot of persuasion from my mum, I found myself knocking on their door. This tall slim lady answered, we had never seen each other before, but without a second's thought, she invited me in. As I walked into their living room, I could see a man who I thought must be her husband, and a young lad with long hair, by their reaction, I don't think they had a clue why I was standing in their living room. The lady went to the bottom of the stairs, and at the top of her voice, shouted, DAVID, the reply came back, WHAT!! Come down, your new friend is here, at this point, I just wanted the floor to swallow me up. Then I heard this thundering noise as David ran down the stairs. This tall lad, with long auburn hair appeared. We both ended up standing in the kitchen talking, well, it was David, doing most of the talking, I was still in shock.

He was asking me what sort of music I liked, and what football team I followed, when I said I didn't follow football, I thought he was going to choke, he then said, he was going to a Stoke City game on Saturday with his mates, and I should go with them. I thought it was me that was supposed to be introducing him to my mates on the estate. Now, I found myself agreeing to go to a football match with his mates. It's at this point, I thought I should do what I had been asked, and take him to meet some of my friends. He seemed up for it, and shouted from the kitchen, Eva, we are going out. I thought, who the bloody hell is Eva, I never thought for a minute he was talking to his mum. Its only over time that I realised, that both David, and his younger brother Graham, both called their parents by their first name, and not mum and dad. I have to say, they were the most loving family. I had never seen anything like it, they would fall out, then give each other a hug, but from that moment on, I was always made to feel welcome in their house, and I loved spending time with them. It was so different to what I was used to. I even became good friends with Graham, the younger brother, but I could never bring myself to call their parents by their first name, it was always Mr or Mrs Walker.

I had about 3 days to get my head around that I was going to go to a football match. I looked in the local paper in a vain attempt to find out more about this football team, but it was all double Dutch to me, apart from that I found out their strip was red and white. That was my full knowledge. The day before the game, I went down to my dad's shed, and got some red paint, and on the back of an old khaki coat, I wrote the words, Stoke City. ☺

A couple of weeks before meeting my new football mate, I had counted my savings in the little tin under my bed. I had managed to save £55 so I spoke to my dad, as I wanted to start looking for a car. A few days later we spotted one for sale in the local newspaper that my dad thought could be ok. We went to look at it, and after a little trial run, it was decided to make an offer, and I got it for £45. I had enough left to pay for the road tax, but I had to borrow the money for the insurance from my dad. My Morris Minor was parked outside our flat next to my dad's car, but I would have to wait another 3 weeks for my 17th birthday before I could have my first lesson. One thing we did, was, to fit indicators on the front and back, as it only had those little amber arms that would shoot out to show which way you were going.

******

On the Saturday morning of my first football match, David had said to be down his house at 10-30, one bit of knowledge that was floating around in my head, was that I thought football games started about 3 o'clock, so I was a bit puzzled as to why we were meeting up so early. From Davids house we walked a bit further down the estate to meet up with the others. I was a bit shocked when we arrived at a house that I knew very well, John was one of my best mates from school. He was the one who I had started my first little business with, the one where we got some hens to try and sell eggs, and, the one who was with me when we lowered ourselves into the scrap yard, and just about escaped before the Alsatian guard dog made a meal of us. The next lad to appear was Harry, also someone I knew. The last one to join us was a lad named Mick, but everyone called him Ugg, he looked a bit different than the rest of us. We all had long hair, but Ugg had very short hair and long sideburns. Now the 5 of us set off walking, we went through the Town and eventually arrived at the railway station, this was a good 3-mile walk. I knew where the football ground was, so I asked my mate why have we just walked 3 miles to get a train to do the last 5 miles, why didn't we just get the bus? My mate just said that Stoke were playing Nottingham Forest, so we are getting the train to Nottingham. It never occurred to me that anyone would travel all that way to watch a game of football. Just as the train was about to pull into the station at Nottingham, David said, when we get off the train, follow me, and run, run!!, I said, run where? Just follow me, we ran, and then jumped over the barrier, and we kept running, apparently, British Rail gave us a free trip to Nottingham. We arrived at the ground, and made our way to the top of the stand. I couldn't believe how many Stoke supporters were there, it must have been close to 3 thousand. After about half an hour, the two teams came out, I was amazed at the noise from all the supporters. As the game got underway, I got quite into it, as Stoke were attacking the opposition goal. I was shouting Go On, Go On, David, looked at me in disbelief, and said, what are you doing? I said, I'm just cheering them on, cheering them on, he said, that's Nottingham Forest you are cheering. How was I supposed to know that Nottingham, were the team in red, and Stoke were playing in their away strip. The game ended and Stoke had won 1-2. We made our way out of the ground, over the Trent bridge and started to walk back to the Railway station. We noticed that a lot of Nottingham Forest supporters were walking on the opposite side of the road. They started shouting at us and making hand gestures that obviously weren't intended to congratulate us on Stoke winning. It's at this point, I started to think it was perhaps

108

not the best idea to put the words Stoke City on the back of my coat. We could see they were starting to cross the road and getting closer to us. We were quite a way off the station so we decided to go into the nearest shop. I think it was Woolworths, we went down the aisle to the back of the shop, but they just followed us, so we went down the next aisle and back outside, it was now time to run. As they were getting closer, I just went into the first shop I came to, inside, I could see a lady behind the counter and another lady sitting on a chair, they just looked at me, then carried on with their conversation. I gave it 5 minutes, then opened the door, I could see someone lying on the floor, but the gang of Forrest supporters had gone. It was Ugg on the floor, he had a cut lip and a bruised ego, but otherwise seemed ok. I helped him up, and we got to the station. The other 3 had made it, and stood waiting for us.

We got back to Longport station, and started to walk back home. This day was starting to become a day of firsts for me, my first football match, and now on our walk home, we stopped off at the British Legion club. So, this was the first time that I had stood at a Bar and ordered a pint of beer. Not sure what I should ask for, my mate suggested I order a pint of Joules bitter. When all 5 of us had got our drinks, the barman said, 'ok lads, off you go'. I followed the others through the double doors at the back of the room and walked into what they called the concert room. It was basically a big room with a small, very low stage at the far end. There were tables and chairs around the room and about half a dozen other people were already in the room who all seemed to know each other. When we first walked in the bar, I noticed that there were only two old men sitting at a table playing Dominos. So, I wondered why we had to go into this back room. One of the lads just said, 'it's because we are all under age, so if the copper's poke their nose through the front door they won't see us'. This club was at the very bottom of the Town and halfway down a grubby side street. It became the go-to place, especially in the colder months. Over the next few weeks, this back room, got a lot more of us underage teenagers meeting up there. It wasn't just lads, there were just as many girls, we all got on, and there was never any trouble. At any one time there could be 20 or 30 of us. We were definitely the club's best customers, and well outnumbered the older customers in the bar.

The landlord was keen on keeping our custom. He installed a jukebox into the back room, for 6d [two and a half pence today] you could play one record, or for 1/- you could play 3 records. There was a new song out at about the same time as this jukebox was installed, it was called Good Vibrations, by a group known as The Beach Boys. This song cost me quite a few shillings, but between all of us, the music from the jukebox kept us entertained most of the night. The girls would be dancing to all this fabulous music, I can't remember the lads dancing, [but I could be wrong]. Very occasionally, the landlord would let local rock bands play in our room, but mainly, they weren't paid, they were just starting up, and mostly, just wanted somewhere to practice. There were quite a few booed of the stage, never to return. I already knew a lot of the boys and girls who would spend their nights in the back room, one of the girls was my neighbour, well, her back garden joined my back garden and we would spend hours just talking over the fence. There were also some of my mates from school, who became part of our ever-increasing gang. These nights were some of the best times of my 1960s life.

The next old photo will give you a little visual picture of the back street of our British Legion Club. The entrance to the club was by the parked car on the right and the lady with the push chair. It's hard to believe that down a grubby back street like this, 30 or so teenagers were having the best of times back in 1966, but you can never judge a book by its cover.

The grubby side street that the British Legion club was in.

Just 50 miles away from this street, there was another club that was halfway down a street that looked very much like this back in 1963. Both clubs looked very similar from the outside, and both clubs ended up being demolished. That is where the similarity ends, our club gave a few teenagers, memories to last a life time. The club 50 miles away gave the world some of the best Rock and Roll music ever, it was called The Cavern Club. I'm not trying, for one minute to compare the two clubs, the Cavern helped to change rock music forever. The only point I'm trying to make, is, looking at the outside of both clubs, you would never believe that they were the place that teenagers could have such a good time.

In the back room of the club, we would talk about music and fashion, but one thing some of the lads would talk about was football. I didn't get too involved in these conversations, but one day, David, came to me and said they had decided to form a football team. The idea was that they would join one of the local Leagues. They had spoken to the Barman, and he agreed they could represent the British Legion club. They started to run football cards to raise money to buy the strip. I wasn't sure why David was telling me this, until one day he came to say they had joined a Sunday league, and had now got the football strip, it was obviously Red and White stripes like the one Stoke City wore. He said that there were 10 of the lads who wanted to play, even I knew there should be 11 to make a full team. He said, we thought you would make a good defender. I did point out that I hadn't got a clue about the rules of football, "all you need to know, he said, is that you must stop the opposition getting close to our goal.

About two weeks later, and after getting myself a pair of football boots, we all met up down the local park. I could see the goal posts at each end, but the pitch between the goal's wasn't exactly the green grass I was expecting, there was more mud than grass, but we did have a linesman [just the one] and a referee. The ref blew his whistle, to start the game. My job was simple, stop them getting near our goal, I started to get fed up with the ref blowing his whistle every time I stopped the opposition. One of our lads came over to me and said, you have got to stop giving free kicks away, well, "I said" I'm just stopping them getting near our goal, yes, "my mate said" but you must tackle them fairly, you can't just keep knocking them over in the mud. I did keep my place in the team, only because they didn't have anyone to replace me.

TIME TO GET BEHIND THE WHEEL

My 17th birthday, at last, I could now drive my car. My dad thought it was best to start my lesson by driving around our estate. This was the first time that I had noticed how narrow the roads were on the estate. Back in 1966 there were probably more people who hadn't got a car than had, but that didn't help when some bugger had parked their car outside their house. My dad insisted, when I was overtaking one of these cars, I used the indicators that we had fitted to my car, bloody hell, I thought, I've got to check my mirror, indicate, slow down, and steer my car past these parked cars, all at the same time.

It must have been hard for my dad, he would leave at 7 o'clock for work and get home at 6, and I would greet him by saying, can we go for a driving lesson tonight. Most nights it was round our estate, practicing parking, hill starts and reversing, but at weekends he would take me around the towns and villages. One Saturday, we were driving around Stoke just as the football match had ended, I was in a queue of traffic when my mates came walking past us, one of them knocked on the car window and shouted," Giza lift" just as the traffic started to move, my dad just said, ignore them. I got some stick from my mates that night down the club.

I got a card through the Post, it said that my test was at 2 o'clock on the 10th of January 1967. Even though I had had all my lessons with my dad, he thought it was a good idea that I should have a driving lesson in my car, but with a driving instructor the hour before my test. After my hour lesson we pulled up at the test station. I will never forget the man taking me for my test, he had horn rimmed glasses, a trilby hat, and a long black rain coat, he looked quite scary. I did the eye test, then 30 minutes later he said, I'm pleased to say you have passed.

Now with my new found freedom, along with some of my mates, we started talking about where we could go. One of them suggested that we should all go on holiday together. We all agreed that this was a brilliant idea, and after a lot of discussion, we decided on Great Yarmouth. It was a 200mile trip, one of my last holidays with my parents and my best mate was at Yarmouth, it had everything a gang of young lads could wish for. The only problem was, there were 6 of us who wanted to go, and my car could only hold 4. One of the lads said he would soon be buying a car, and as it would be 6 months before we went, he had plenty of time to pass his test. I went home and asked my mum for the address of the caravan park we had stayed at in Caister-on-sea, which was about 2 miles from Yarmouth centre. The best thing about this caravan site was that it was right by the beach, and next to a pub. This pub had a brilliant name, it was called The Never Turn Back.

Now, I had to send a letter to the caravan site explaining what we wanted, and how many of us would be going. They sent a letter back with the price of renting the caravan for two weeks, I then had to send a postal order covering the deposit. This was the slow drawn-out process that we had to go through back in the 60s. It could drag out over a couple of weeks. Today we could probably do all of that in less than an hour.

******

We had become good mates with quite a few of the girls who would spend their nights in the back room of the club with us. Occasionally, I would ask one of the girls if she wanted to go to the cinema with me, if she said yes, then we would meet up the following night. There was never any question of us going Dutch, as they call it today, I would pay for both of us and even share a bag of chips on the way home. "I knew how to treat a lady." It was early days with my dating experiences. It was a bit like an apprenticeship,

I remember when I was about 14, along with my best mate Bryn, we had a double date with two girls who were sisters. It was at a time when they were just transforming from Aliens, and we boys, started to look at them in a totally different way. These dates were just sitting on a bench on the park that we had grown up playing on, we would be just holding hands and talking. My first romantic gesture came one night, when the 4 of us were sitting on the park looking up at a perfectly clear sky, I noticed a star formation that looked like a big saucepan, [its only years later that I found out it was Ursa Major or better known as the Great Bear] but on that night it was a big saucepan. I said to the girl who was my date, when you get home, if we both look up at the stars {the saucepan} at 10 o'clock we can both think of each other, [you must admit, from a 14year old, that was very romantic] the next time we met, she handed me a little note, that said, "I looked up at the stars, did you?" I just said, 'yes'.

I spoke to my mate recently, and he remembers the two girls, but sadly, we can't remember how it ended. My next date was with a girl whose parents ran a pub down the lane from the play park, again it was just holding hands, and I would walk her home from the park down a very dark country lane. The walk back up that lane on my own was scary, So, you can see my apprenticeship had started. The girls who I took out on a date from the club, mostly to the cinema, were part of my dating experience. One of the

116

more exciting places to take a girl on a date, was a night club that opened at the top end of our town in 1965. Again, this club was in a grotty back street, but it turned out to be one of the go-to places, not only from the locals of Stoke, but from all around the country. The club was called The Golden Torch and this club attracted all the top performers, not only from the U.K but even some of the top acts from America. Who would have thought our little town of Tunstall could attract such talent.

One of the lads from down the Legion club had started to go out with a girl who was a student nurse, she spent Monday to Friday living in, at the Hospital, but when she came home at the weekend's, she would bring one of her mates with her, and the 4 of us would go out on Saturday night. It was like a blind date for me. Each Saturday she would bring a different girl for my date. This happened about 4 times and these student nurses weren't as shy or reserved as most of the girls I had dated from the Legion club.

I was never sure whether it was a good thing that she brought a different friend each Saturday for my date, or, if the girl from the previous week didn't fancy a second date with me.

*****

Just after we had decided that 6 of us should go on holiday together, my mate managed to buy a car, well, it was a Minnie Van, but that was fine, we could get 4 in my car and 2 in his Van, and we could all put our luggage in the back of the Van. Like me, he was going to get his dad to give him driving lessons.

Fast forward two months, and my mate took his driving test, and failed, but we still had 4 months to go for the holiday, so, plenty of time.

Along with David, I was sitting in the Legion club one night with two other lads, they were telling us that they were starting a Rock band and they asked David and me if we wanted to join them. The first thing that went through my mind, was, the last time I had suggested forming a band with 3 of my mates, it hadn't ended well. First, none of us back then had got the money to buy guitars or drums, and my singing audition turned out to be a bit embarrassing. So, my first question to the two lads asking us to join their band, was, can you sing? they both answered, yes. One of the lads played the Bass guitar and the other played Lead guitar, they were looking for someone to play Drums and someone to play Rhythm guitar.

******

One of my Birthday presents at the age of 13 was an acoustic guitar, at the time I thought it was wonderful, but looking back, it was a three-quarter sized guitar with nylon strings. I think, even a good guitar player would have struggled to get a good sound out of it, but back then, to me it was a guitar. My dad had seen an advert in the local paper offering guitar lessons, but to get to these lessons we had to travel about 5 miles from home. The lessons were on a Friday night and lasted half an hour, my dad would wait outside in his car, and my first lesson was spent with the teacher trying his best to tune this rubbish guitar. The following week, he started to show me how to play Old MacDonald Had a Farm. I wasn't impressed, this wasn't the Rock and Roll music I was hoping for, but I went home and practiced, one thing about this tune, was, it could be played on just one string. My mum and dad were very supportive, they even thought I should practice in my bedroom, so I wouldn't get distracted by the TV. My third lesson, and the teacher thought I should perfect Old

MacDonald before moving onto something else. I didn't bother going back for a fourth lesson

******

Back at the Legion club, both of us said we would love to join their band, thankfully, David said that he had always wanted to play Drums. I had to admit that my guitar skills weren't up to much, but Pete, the lead guitarist said he was happy to teach me. The following Saturday along with David we made our way to Hanley [the main shopping centre]. I knew some very good second-hand shops where you could get almost anything from. The first we visited, was a big double fronted shop, it was in Hope St, and run by a very flamboyant lady named Rosina Ward. It was from this shop that my dad had had many bargains, including the TV that we now had.

Now with all the young lads starting Rock bands and very quickly packing in, these shops were full of musical instruments. As we stood looking in the window, I could see a red Electric guitar, inside the shop, I found an Amplifier to go with the guitar, and after a little negotiation, I came out with the Guitar and Amp, but there were no Drum Kits for David. The next shop we went to had 3 kits set up, David chose one, but the problem was that it was too big to get in my car, and he was a few pounds short of the price the shop wanted. We went home, and David borrowed the extra money from his mum, and got a friend with a van to go back with him to collect his Drum Kit.

It was easy for me to carry my guitar down to Pete's house and start to learn a few chords, but David had to set his Drum Kit up in his bedroom to start to practice. The following day I went down Davids to see how he was getting on with his drums. As I walked down the path I

119

could hear him hard at work practicing, when I knocked on the door, the first thing his mum said to me was, thank goodness you are here, I hope you have come to take him out. To be fair to David, I thought he sounded quite good.

We did, for a brief second, think of asking the barman down the Legion club if we could practice in the back room, but we soon put that idea to bed, the stick we would get from our mates wouldn't have helped.

I remembered, when I use to walk home from school, there was an old Scout building, that I thought would be ideal. I went and asked the caretaker, and he said we could use it twice a week, Mondays, and Thursdays, from 7 o'clock to 9-30, we would have to pay 15/- [75pence today] for the two nights, and there was a store room that we could lock up all our instruments in.

After a few trips in my car, I managed to get all our things up to the room, including two trips with Davids Drum Kit, there was no room for anyone else in my car, so I had to unload it all myself. I got so excited on our first practice night, this is something I had wanted to do since 1963, now in 1967 we set up like a proper Rock Band. The first song we played was Louie Louie by a group called The Kingsmen, Pete and Ray stood at the mike, Dave behind his drums and me with my guitar, it was a simple song to play with just 3 chords and an easy drum pattern. By the end of the night, we had got something that we all thought was a good sound.

One thing I did on that first night, was, to take my tape recorder, just so we could hear what we sounded like.

****

When I started to put these memories together, I went through hundreds of photos and letters that my mum had saved, also the photos, letters, and the odd Diary that over

120

the years we had accumulated. I can't tell you the hours I have spent looking for a certain photo to go along with a story. One thing I did, was to get my old tape recorder down from the loft, and while I was looking through the photos, I played some of the old recordings that I had made from the 60s. One of those recordings was of our first night learning to play Louie Louie. Listening to that recording, the acoustics in the room weren't the best, but to be able to hear the 4 of us,55 years on from that night, playing that song was quite emotional for me.

*****

After my first football game following Stoke City away at Nottingham Forest, and now being part of the team playing in the local football leagues, representing the Legion club, I started to get quite interested in football. Along with some of my mates I started to go to many of Stoke's home games and a few away games.

In 1967 Stoke were in what was called the First Division, [today it would be the Premiership] so we would play some of the top teams in the country. I started to understand the rules of the game, something that had let me down on my first game watching Stoke at Nottingham Forest and playing my first game in the local league.

One Stoke player that got my attention was named Morris Setters, he played in the defence, and played in the same position that I was expected to play in our amateur games down the local park. He was a tough no nonsense player, and unlike me, he could tackle a player without the Ref constantly blowing his whistle. Stoke at the time had some excellent players, one of their star signings was Gordon Banks, who was a goalkeeper, he was the England goalkeeper through-out the 1966 World Cup, and joined Stoke the following season, [my first season as a football supporter]. We also got to see some of the best players to play against Stoke. One game that sticks in my mind, was, Stoke, playing at home against Manchester United, it was a Wednesday night game, the ground was packed with over 50 thousand supporters. Along with my mates I stood in the Boothen End, one of the United players got the ball around the half way line and despite the best attempts of 4 of the Stoke defenders, he went past them as though they weren't there, and scored a magical goal, his name was George Best. He was just 21 at the time.

SOMETIMES FATE
TAKES A HAND

[APRIL 3rd 1967]

I started to look forward to our practice nights, playing in a band with my 3 mates was becoming the highlight of my week. I would take my guitar home with me, and go down to Pete's house over the weekend, and he would teach me new chords that would go with the next songs we would be playing. Unlike school, this was homework I enjoyed doing.

Usually, on Monday and Thursday nights I would call for David and we would meet up with Pete and Ray for our practice night, but on this particular Monday I was having a problem with my car. My dad said that he would have a look at it, so we decided to walk. I didn't want to miss this practice night, as we were going to have a go at one of my favourite

songs, it was Twist and Shout, by The Beatles, again it was just 3 chords, [for anyone that's interested, the chords are E, A, and B]. The only problem with this song was that someone would sing the lead and two others would sing the replies, but we only had Pete and Ray who could sing. Pete looked at me, and said, you will have to do the replies bit with Ray. Now, I don't know if you remember, but as a 13year old, I did a duet with Cliff Richards on the radio, and I asked my mum if she thought I sounded like Cliff, and she quite bluntly, said, No Son, you don't, but she did give me a glimmer of hope, by saying, maybe it's because your voice is breaking. Now at seventeen, my voice had well and truly broken, so, with my mum's words ringing in my head, I stood at the Mike with Ray. I sang those replies as quietly as I could, almost miming, but it was decided that, perhaps it was best if just Ray did it on his own. To be honest, I didn't care, no matter what, I was playing along with Twist and Shout, it was better than Old MacDonald Had a Farm.

At the end of our little practice session, Dave and me started to walk back home. As we came onto our estate, we could see 4 people standing under a lamp post talking, it was 2 girls and 2 boys. I recognised one of the girls, her name was Eunice Elsby, her parents were friends of my mum and dad. We had even spent some time together on a holiday in Great Yarmouth. I had seen the other two lads before, but I didn't really know them that well, and I couldn't remember seeing the other girl at all.

Since David had moved onto our estate, he had noticed Eunice. The conversation went like this.

David, can you see the blond girl over there.
Me, yes, that's Eunice,
David, do you know her then?
Me, yes, why?
David, I wouldn't mind taking her out on a date.
Me, well, she's nice.
David, let's go over and talk to them.
Me, I'm not sure, they are with those two lads.
David, let's go over to them.
Me, and what am I supposed to do?
David, well, the other girl looks ok, you can ask her out.
Me, Thanks, what if the two lads are their boyfriends?
David, come on, let's do it.
Me, bloody hell Dave, I don't even know the other girl.

Before I knew it, we were walking over the road to them, David whispering to me, you start talking to them first, as you know one of them.

Me, in my most sarcastic voice. Thanks Dave.

As we got to them, I just said Hi to Eunice, and asking if she was ok, the two lads didn't seem too impressed with us joining them, but thankfully, they decided to go, leaving the 4 of us talking.

It didn't take Dave long before he asked Eunice if she wanted to go for a walk, Eunice just said, ok, and off they went. That left me just standing under a lamp post with the other girl.

Over the last 18 months or so, the girls I had taken out were mates from down the club, or the student nurses, who were like a blind date, but that would be the 4 of us going for a drink or going to the cinema.

Even though I had lived on the estate for 12 years, I can't ever remember seeing this girl before, and now we were just standing there together. I thought she was very attractive, and I found myself just saying, "do you want to go for a walk," fully expecting her to say No, but to my amazement, she said Yes. We walked in the opposite direction to David and Eunice, and very soon we were talking as if we had known each other for years. I put my arm around her shoulder, not quite knowing what reaction I would get, but she just put her arm around my waist. Part of our very short walk took us along a path at the back of the estate. We had only been together for about 30 minutes, but I had never felt like this before with any of the girls I had been with, we stopped on this track, and I kissed her.

We got back onto the estate, and as we came around the corner, and back to the place we had started our walk, she said, take your arm from around me, I asked why? She just said, that's my mum standing there, I looked up to see a lady standing near to the lamp post. I kept my arm around her until we reached a very stern looking mum, who said, "what time do you call this". As they walked down the drive, I said, good night, to both of them, and the mum gave me a very sharp, "Good Night" reply. Apparently, she should have been in at 10-30 it was now 10-45. The road I lived in was directly opposite their house, which made it even more amazing that I couldn't remember seeing her before, but on my short walk home I thought, with the reaction from her mum I had blown any chance of seeing her again.

I went to work the next day as normal, but kept thinking of this girl I had seen for probably not much more than 30 minutes the night before.

When I got home from work, my dad had managed to sort the problem out with my car, so, I went to pick David up, and we went down the Legion club. I asked him how he had got on with Eunice, he just said, it was ok. I told him the story about my night with the other girl. On our way home, David suggested, that we should see if they were there again. As we got near to the lamp post we couldn't see anyone, but I now knew where she lived. I pulled up outside, we sat there for a couple of minutes, David, then suggested that I Peep my horn, to see if I could get her attention, so I did, about 3 or 4 times. Not long after a man appeared behind the gate, halfway down the drive, this wasn't something I was expecting, but I wound my window down and started to say, Is, then I realised I

126

hadn't asked her what her name was, so, I quickly spluttered, is your daughter in, he put his arm over the gate pointing at me and said, SWINE OFF.

I did as he had asked, and drove off as fast as my little Morris Minor would go. I dropped David off, then went home. I thought, well, if I hadn't blown my chances of seeing her again the night before with her mum, I had definitely done it this time with her dad. The following night I decided to walk down to see David. I lived at the top of Westbourne Drive, it's shaped like a crescent, so there were two ways out, one was a slightly shorter way, but I decided to take the other way, this took me down the road that went towards the house that the girl lived in. As I got closer to their house, I could see someone moving in the living room, now, after my brief encounters with her parents, I knew her mum had short wavy hair, and I had noticed her dad had grey hair. Whoever it was in the living room had long dark hair, so I took a chance and sort of half waved. By the time I got to the end of the road, she came walking up the drive and across the road towards me. She was smiling, so I thought all was not lost. I started to tell her about my encounter with her dad, she laughed, and said she knew. She told me that she was in the kitchen making her dad a mug of Ovaltine. When he came back in, and said, I have just told those two lads to swine off. She said, she had poured his drink down the sink. After a heated discussion with her mum and dad they had agreed that I could see her again, but only if I came and knocked on the door at a reasonable time.

We went for a short walk, and it felt great to be with her again, at last I found out her name was Pat. As we

127

walked back to her house, I said that I would call round the next night and knock on her door.

The following night was Thursday, and our practice night. I knew if I went it would be too late to go knocking on her door. I couldn't get it wrong for 3 nights on the trot, so I told my mates I couldn't make our practice night. So, at 7 O'clock I went and knocked on their back door. Pat opened the door, and just said, hi, come in. As I walked into the kitchen, I could see her mum at the sink, and what turned out to be her sister, who was ironing some clothes. Pats mum asked me if I wanted a cup of tea, and i was told to sit down, I could see a small stool in the corner of the room, I sat down with my cup of tea. I don't know if you remember those clothes dryers that hung from the ceiling and you could lower them down on a pully, well Pats sister started to lower this dryer down, and it was right in front of me, so all I could see was a row of clothes and legs moving around on the other side.

I heard a car pulling down the drive, and then a man's legs appeared under the row of clothes. It didn't take a genius to work out who they belonged to, then, I could hear the squeaky noise of the pully taking the clothes dryer back up to the ceiling, my cover was about to be blown. The man who had told me to "Swine Off" two nights before was now standing in front of me. I gave him a very awkward smile, he reached into his pocket and pulled out a packet of Park Drive cigarettes and offered me one, I just thanked him, and he walked off into the living room without saying a word, what a relief.

Looking back, they weren't being nasty towards me, they were just protecting their daughter. Pat, just 4 weeks previous to us meeting, had had her 16th birthday, and she was still at school, so their reaction was understandable.

The man who told me to Swine Off, eventually, became my best friend, and was one of the nicest men you could ever wish to meet.

Harry loved his cars, he would jokingly say, the ashtray is full, it's time to swap the car. No second-hand cars for Harry.

Now I was spending my nights with Pat, going down the Legion Club was becoming few and far between. Even though I had had many happy nights down the Club, taking Pat there wasn't something I thought was right, she was only just 16.

I know I was only 16 when I started going in the Club, but that was my choice, and if the police had paid us a visit, I would only have myself to blame. Now, if I put Pat in that situation, I dread to think what her mum and dad would say. Being in trouble with the police was one thing, being in trouble with Pat's mum and dad was on a different level.

I was still going to my practice nights on Monday and Thursday with my mates, but I would still call at Pat's for the last half hour or so

Not long after we had started seeing each other, Pat told me she was going to a Rock Concert with Eunice, when I asked who she was going to see, she said, it was Engelbert Humperdinck and Jimi Hendrix. I said, wow, that will be brilliant, Jimi Hendrix, is one of my guitar heroes.

Oh, Pat said, I'm not interested in him, I'm going to see Engelbert.

Most nights we would go for a walk or if it was raining, spend the night in Pat's kitchen, playing music and cards. At weekends we would go a run out in my car.

I mentioned to Pat about my planned holiday in Great Yarmouth with my mates in August, she said she was also going on holiday at the same time with her mum and dad, they had just bought a small caravan in Mid Wales at a place called Llanidloes. The idea was they would spend some weekends there, and, also, their main summer holiday.

It was now May, and my mate, who was trying to pass his driving test in time for our holiday, was due to take his second test. When I got home from work, I went straight down his house with my fingers crossed, hoping, he had passed. The only way we could go on this holiday, was, if we had my car and his Mini Van, as 6 lads in one car with all our luggage just wouldn't fit. As I walked into his house, I didn't have to ask, the look on his face was enough to say he had failed, but we still had just over two months to go, so hopefully third time lucky.

Not the best photo, but it's the only one I have of Eunice on the left, and Pat, at about the same time that we met.

I found this photo of Pat's mum, Kath, cutting their hedge. She wasn't smiling the first night I met her. She is also next to the lamp post that Pat and Eunice were standing under, with the two boys, when David talked me into going over to them to see if he could get a date with Eunice.

This aerial shot is of the top end of our estate, the **M** mark was my house, the **E** mark was Eunice's house, the **P** mark was Pat's house and the **D** mark was David's house, and if I'm being ultra-romantic, if you look to the top left of the photo the **X** was on the path that we had our first kiss.

SHARING MY BED
WITH A FEW OTHERS

Now that the weather was getting better, Pat's parents decided it was time to start going to their caravan.

They had been going to this place for quite a few years. Harry [Pat's dad] loved fishing, and they started by going camping in the field about 3 miles from Llanidloes, next to the River Severn, but now their caravan was up in the hills, in a beautiful spot that had fantastic views looking down the valley. The caravan sat in a small corner of a field next to a Farm house, but the field was not owned by the farm.

Now I was spending a lot of time with Pat and her family, they asked me if I would like to go to the caravan with them at the weekend. Harry, had quite a big car, it was a Zepher 6 and brand new. Along with Pat, Harry, and Kath there were also Pats sister, Ann who was 2 years younger and her brother Malcolm who was 10, so, it was quite cramped with 4 of us squeezed into the back seat. Occasionally, Pat and me would follow behind in my car, but mostly, it was all of us in Harry's car.

We would set off around 6pm, it was about a 90-mile trip, so, we would stop off half way at a pub, that was aptly named the Halfway House. We would arrive at the caravan around 9pm. The caravan was quite small, but it had been arranged that I could sleep in a spare room at the farm house next to the caravan. They had become good friends with Kath and Harry, so, on my first night, I was introduced to the couple in the farmhouse. As I walked into their living room I could see, an old man sitting by an open fire in the dark. The lady handed me a candle, she said, we don't have any electric in the house, so we have to use candles. She then showed me to my room, it was on the ground floor and just off the living room. As I walked into the bedroom all I could see was a single bed, there was nothing else in the room, apart from a nail on the back of the door to hang my clothes on. The only window was about 2ft square, and had a piece of sacking hanging in front of it as a curtain. I climbed into bed and blew my candle out, and placed it on the floor. I was struggling to get off to sleep, and after about 30 minutes, I could feel something moving at the bottom of my bed, I kicked my feet, and for a few minutes it stopped, but then it started again. It didn't take me long to work out I was sharing my bed with a few mice, well, I hoped it was mice and not something a bit bigger. It was absolutely pitch black in the room. I couldn't see a thing. It was a very long night, and I had to do it all again the following night.

Fortunately, not long after my first visit to the caravan, Kath and Harry decided to part exchange their small caravan for a much bigger one, so now, my sleeping arrangements were much better. A good night's sleep, topped off with Kath's full English breakfast made these weekends magical.

By the summer of 1967 Pat left school, she had had a Saturday job working at a hair dressing salon. It was long hours, with very little pay, but Pat would save her wages, so that she could buy things like pop magazines, or some clothes that were in fashion, but perhaps her mum wouldn't think necessary.

At school, one of the lessons was typing, something that she was interested in, but for whatever reason the school decided, she couldn't take part in this class, so, in her lunch break, she would go to this class room, and in time taught herself to type. Now, with this skill, Pat managed to first

135

get a job at English Electric, in the typing pool, and just by chance I was sent on a job, building a Lloyds Bank. It was right opposite the offices that Pat worked in, she was on the top floor, and I would keep looking up at the window, just to get a glimpse of her. Every now and then, she would look out of the window and give me a wave. Now, you can look at this in two ways, [1] you may be thinking, what a soppy sod, or [2] you may think, this is young love. I don't mind which one you choose.

It was in this office that Pat met Eileen, she became a friend for life, they ring each other 2 or 3 times a week, each phone call can last well over an hour. At the end of the phone call, I will say, is Eileen ok. what did she have to say? The reply will be, oh, not much.

Unlike me, Pat, could and should have gone on to further education, but in 1967, most working-class families of our generation thought we should go out to work, to contribute to the family income.

******

It was now getting close to our holiday, and my mate was about to take his 3rd driving test, it was make or break, if he failed this time, it would be almost impossible for all 6 lads to go on this holiday to Great Yarmouth. We had no way of knowing if he had passed until we got home from work. So, like last time, I finished work and went straight down his house. I walked into his living room to see him sitting there and not looking very happy, but he couldn't keep his sad face expression up for long, and with a big smile, said, I passed.

The day had arrived, the holiday was booked for Saturday 5th of August 1967, but we were excited, and decided to go on the Friday night and get most of the way. We thought that if we slept in our cars with just a few miles to go, then we could be in Great Yarmouth early on Saturday morning and make a full day of it.

Before we set off, I went down to Pats house to say my goodbyes, she was also going on holiday the next day with her family for two weeks at their caravan in Llanidloes. We decided we would send each other a letter every other day. Pat gave me the address of the farmhouse next to their caravan, and I gave Pat the address of our camp site. It was only when I left her, that I started to wonder what I had agreed to, my writing was scruffy and my spelling was atrocious, [even now, I just had to look up how to spell atrocious!]

We set off, 4 of us in my car, and 2 in my mates mini-van. We managed to travel about 150 miles, when my car fuel gauge was showing empty. We found a petrol station, but it was closed for the night, the sign said, it opened at 9am. We decided [well we had no choice] to spend the night by the garage. We eventually got to Yarmouth the next day about 12 O'clock. Looking at our caravan, I think the site had worked out that it was 6 teenage boys staying in the van, it had definitely seen better days, but we didn't care. We unpacked our things, then went to the pub next to the site. It was a beautiful day, blue skies and hot, we spent the afternoon on the beach, then we went into Yarmouth, the first job was to find a fish and chip shop, we were 6 very hungry lads. The theatres along the front were advertising some of the top pop groups of the day, some of them were for one night only, so choosing the ones to book up to see wasn't easy.

Each morning we went to a café next to our site for breakfast, I can't remember any of us cooking any meals in the caravan. Tuesday was my 18th birthday, I went to the camp shop, and collected my post, there were a few birthday cards and a letter from Pat, in part of her letter, she told me that John, the son of the farmer who owned the land that their caravan was on, was starting to spend time with them.

On my birthday we decided to visit one of the Norfolk Broads and hire a boat, sailing up the Broads and stopping off at a pub, it was turning out to be a brilliant day. At night we went to the pub next to the site, it was more like a club rather than a pub, and they had a group playing in the concert room. At last, I could drink a pint and it was legal, the group were quite good, but Tommy one of my mates was a much better singer than the lad the group had, Tommy had been the lead singer to quite a few of our local Rock Bands, so we were encouraging him to get up and do a couple of songs with the Band, he wasn't too keen, and the Band didn't seem interested, but we kept pushing him to get on stage. In the end, Tommy and the Band agreed that he would do a couple of songs with them, after his first song he got a great round of applause from the packed room. Tommy was a showman, and what a show he put on that night, he spent the rest of the night fronting the Band, much to the annoyance of the Bands singer.

I had too much to drink that night, mostly because my mates kept getting me drinks for my birthday. It was only a few yards [meters] from the pub to our van, but for whatever reason, I never made it back to my bed, I opened my eyes the following morning curled up on the beach, just as the sun was popping up over the North Sea. I made my way back to the van, and as I opened the door, the smell was like walking into a Brewery. Our 6-birth van had two beds that were each side of the table, a double bed that you pulled down each night, and then there was a little room that had bunk beds in it, I was on the bottom bunk, and that's where I stayed until about 2 o'clock.

138

I had only been really drunk once before, I somehow made my way home, but couldn't find my key. As we lived in a flat, I looked up, I could see a light on, so I shouted, Mum, I've lost my key, I did this about three times, eventually I could hear my mum, shouting in a hushed voice, what are you doing, be quiet, you will wake up the neighbours, the next thing, she was at the door, she just said, Get In, and go to bed.

The following morning my mum asked me what I was playing at the night before, I said, I had lost my key, and I could see the light on, I was just trying to get your attention, she said, we were in bed, you woke me up, when I looked out of the window, you were standing under the lap post looking up at the light, shouting, I've lost my key.

That was one of those times when you wake up the next day and say, Never Again. [well, apparently not]

By the middle Saturday, I was starting to run out of money, so I went to the phone box on the site. Not many people had telephones back then, but fortunately, our next-door neighbour had just had a phone installed, and my mum had given me their number before we set out, it was just in case of emergencies. Well, I thought running out of money was an emergency, so I rang our neighbours and asked if I could speak to my mum, they then had to go and knock on our door and get her to come to the phone. I explained to her my problem, she said, I will talk to your dad, ring back in an hour. When I rang back my mum said they would send me some money, but obviously they thought I couldn't be trusted with having all the money in one go, so it was decided that they would send ten shillings [50p] each day by post to the camp site office. Thankfully, the post office, were very   reliable back then, you could post a letter one day and it would be delivered the next day. So, each day I would collect the envelope with my money in, also any letters from Pat. The lady at the camp office said she had never known anyone have so much post sent to them.

We had both done as promised, so it was nice to get my letters from Pat, telling me about her holiday, I must say her letters were far more interesting than the badly written scrawl I was sending in return. In one of her letters, she told me that John, the son of the farmer who owned the land their caravan was on, was spending a lot of time with them, and it was obvious that he fancied Ann, [Pats sister]. They were both quite shy, so Pat decided to give them a helping hand, and locked the two of them in the caravan together to get them talking. It worked, but once they went back home poor John had a 180mile round trip to continue his courtship with Ann.

The middle Saturday [12th August 1967] we all sat on the beach talking about the pop charts, and what would be number 1# on Sunday, I thought it would be The Beatles, who were number one at the time with a song called "All You Need Is Love", but Mick, [Ugg] thought it would be a song by an American singer named Scott McKenzie, it was a good song with a very long title, "San Francisco [be sure to wear some flowers in your hair].

The summer of 1967 was known as the summer of Peace, Love and Flower Power, I had a bet with Ugg, as to which song would be number one. It was agreed that whoever lost would have to walk down the seafront of Yarmouth covered in flowers [Flower Power].

The next day the song with the long title had knocked the Beatles off the number one spot, so, off we all went to the far end of Yarmouth. The council flower beds were in full bloom so we had plenty of colourful flowers to choose from. My mile long walk covered in flowers was met with a lot of interest and finger pointing by the hundreds of people walking along the seafront.

Our two weeks holiday was coming to an end. One thing I remember, was, we had beautiful weather from start to finish, with blue skies. We had had a brilliant holiday, but now it was time to hand back the keys to our caravan and start our trip back home. It must have been an uneventful trip, as I can't remember much about the journey home. I first dropped off Bryn, then Ugg, and finally Dave, I then drove round the corner to see if Pat had got back from their holiday. Their car was in the drive, so I knocked on the door, it felt so good to see her again, we sat in the kitchen swapping holiday stories. One of the things that shocked me was that my mum and dad had decided to go a run out to their caravan unannounced, and spent the day with them. This was just before the end of the holiday, so she didn't have time to tell me in her letters.

This photo and the one on the next page were both taken in
the field by the caravan in Llanidloes.

Pat washing my hair, with her brother looking on!

Just look at the beautiful views down the valley

Kath on the left then Malcom, Harry, Ann, and Pat.

These were beautiful memorable times in my life.

PHOTOS FROM OUR LADS' HOLIDAY

Tommy, [holding the ball], he was the one who went on stage to sing a couple of songs and ended up singing with the Band for the rest of the night. In the centre of the photo, my lifelong friend, Bryn. Next to Dave's Legs is Ugg, [Mick] who I had the bet with as to what would be number 1# in the pop charts. I managed to colourize this old black and white photo, but I left the rest as they were.

I thought it would be nice to get Pat a present, Ugg is modelling it inside the caravan! I'm trying to get to grips with the fastener, and I'm not sure what Dave was thinking of doing with his hand!

One of my mates suggested I should go into the shop and cup both my hands and ask if they had a Bra about this size, the shop assistant just smiled and said I'm sure we have.

Unfortunately, the photos are of a poor quality, the only camera we had was an old Kodak Brownie 127. I think the roll of film took 12 photos, then we would take the film to the camp shop to get it developed.

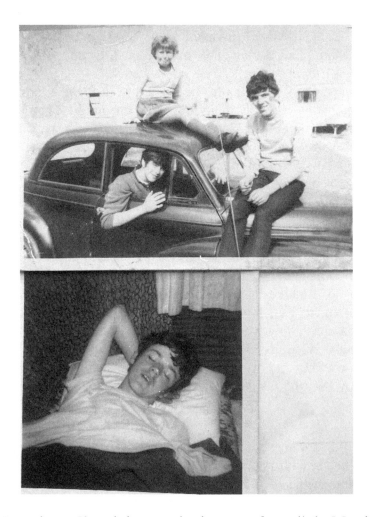

Top photo, I'm sitting on the bonnet of my little Morris Minor, my mate Bryn is at the wheel. The girl was from our neighbouring caravan I can't remember her name, but her parents were Sheffield Utd supporters, so there was a lot of football banter. Bottom photo, Dave, recovering from a heavy night.

My life in 1967/68 revolved around, pop music, fashion, my hair, looking in the mirror [a lot] and Pat, not necessarily in that order.

Even though the Beatles were a big influence on my fashion, by 1967/68 their look was changing. Their hair was getting much longer and they had beards and moustaches, not something that I intended to follow. By August of 1967 their manager Brian Epstein tragically died. They never seemed quite the same after his death, although, even before that, they were becoming, for want of a better word, weird. They travelled on train to Bangor in Wales for a seminar with some Biblical looking figure that went by the name of Maharishi Mahesh Yogi, who was promoting Transcendental Meditation. Then in 1968 they followed him to Rishikesh in Northern India, and lived in an Ashram, it was, I suppose, a bit like a Hippy Commune. Apparently, they were very productive at this time, writing many new songs, but all this weird and way-out lifestyle was way beyond my pay grade, and I was happy to hang on to my 1964/65 fashion look.

******

By the summer of 1968 we were still spending some weekends with Pats parents at their caravan. One weekend in June we decided to follow Harry and go to the caravan in my car. It was on this fateful trip that my car broke down, and the cost of repairing it or towing it back home would cost more than my car was worth, so we spoke to George, the farmer, who's land Pats parents had their caravan on, he said he would tow it to a safe place with his tractor.

We all travelled back home in Harry's car, leaving my little Morris Minor behind.

147

I felt lost without it, and, also, we had arranged a holiday in August, with my mate Bryn and his girlfriend Vivien, so, without a car there was not going to be a holiday.

Just after we got back my dad bought a new car, it was a Ford Zephyr Zodiac, and he said I could buy his old Consul 375 for £100. I loved that car, but the only problem was, I didn't have £100☹, Eventually it was agreed that I could pay for it weekly, for £2 a week, over 12 months. This was still a lot of money to me, but it meant I could have my dream car, and, also, we could still go on holiday with Bryn and Viv.

Because none of us had much money, Pat had asked her parents if we could use their caravan for our holiday. The problem with this idea was, that Pats mum, didn't think it was appropriate for two teenage boys to share a caravan with two teenage girls. Eventually we found the answer, friends of Pats parents also had a caravan, it was just a mile down the road and they agreed that we could use their van. So, Bryn and me could stay in that van and Pat and Viv could stay in the other. This sounded like a good compromise, as Bryn and me thought that once we were there, we could rearrange the sleeping arrangements, well, how wrong we were. The girls made it clear that they were 100% with Pats mum, so each night Bryn and me said our goodnights to the girls, and made our way to the other caravan. Regardless of our devious intentions, we spent the two weeks travelling in style to different places in my new car and had a good holiday.

Just a foot note to this holiday, on our first day I spotted my old Moris Minor. George had towed it to a field, and it was now being used as a dog kennel! ☹□

Pat and me giving the Consul 375 a wash, this was the car I was paying my dad £2 a week for, we felt so proud of it. You can see my dad's new car parked in front.

Bryn and Viv, at around the time we went on holiday with them, to Llanidloes in 1968, when Pat's mum insisted, we should have two caravans, as she didn't think it was right that two teenage boys should share a caravan with the girls. [a very wise woman!!] Bryn and myself have been mates now for over 70 years, and along with Pat and Viv, we still meet up regularly for days out and at least once a month have what we call a F.N.S [that's a, "Friday Night Special"] where we have a drink, play our favourite music from the 60s, laugh [a lot], and as the night wears on, sing along to the songs, as by this time we don't care what we sound like. Two very special friends.

The Sunday after we got back from our holiday, we went a run out to Manifold Vally, it was a lovely sunny day and as we walked along the valley, we started talking about getting engaged. We had decided that we wouldn't get married until we had our own house. This was quite a bold idea back in 1968. The thought of getting married and then moving into one of our parent's houses until we could get a council house filled us with dread, but this is what many young married couples would do back then.

The following weekend we went to the Halifax Building Society, and opened a joint account. We chose a Building Society rather than a Bank as we were told we had a better chance of getting a Mortgage if we saved with them. Then we sat in Pats kitchen doing the maths. Obviously, we would need a deposit for whatever house we bought. Then there was the cost of the wedding and reception, the list went on and on. I thought at this rate it would take years of saving, so, some tough decisions had to be made. First, I took my guitar and sold it back to the second-hand shop, then the hardest decision of all, as much as I loved my new car, I told my dad that I couldn't afford it, so I gave it back after just 6 weeks, my dad did ok out of it and sold it for £150.

So it was back to walking, and on one of my walks, I went past the bus stop that from the age of 5, I would get the bus for school. By this bus stop there was a very wide drive and at the bottom I could see 4 or 5 ice cream vans parked by a building. I decided to go and ask if I could take one of these vans out at weekends. The interview took about as long as my apprentice joiner interview, he just said, have you got a full driving licence, yes, I said, ok, you can take that van out, pointing to one. These ice cream vans sold the soft ice cream, not the same as the ice cream that I had been used too. In fact, the vans had the name across the front, "Mr

Softy". I had a crash course in how it worked, first, you had a gallon can of cream, and you poured it into the top of the machine, then you added 2 gallons of water and switched it on, after about 15 minutes it was ready to go. I asked when did he want me to start, he just looked at me and said, as we have put the ice cream in the machine it needs to go out Now. So, with less than one hour training, I was an ice cream man. I did ask what route I should take, his answer was, just drive round all the side streets until you have sold out. He pointed to a switch and said that plays the chimes to let everyone know you are coming. The tune I was used to was Greensleeves, but my van played The Pied Piper. I only got paid on what I sold, so off I went. I thought, as I lived on a big council estate that was a good place to start. After a few splutters of ice cream shooting out of the machine because I was pulling the lever too fast, I soon got the hang of it. It took me about 3 hours to get to the top of the estate. I pulled up outside Pats house. The last time I did this I peeped my car horn and got told to swine off by her dad, this time playing the Pied Piper jingle no one came out, so, I went and knocked on her door. I told her what I had done. I don't think she could take in what I was telling her, as we walked up the drive and she saw the van, she just said, you weren't joking then. I opened the van door and we both climbed in and off we went. After about an hour Pat decided she wanted a go at filling the cornets, so now I had a glamorous assistant. After we had sold all our ice cream, I dropped Pat off and took the van back. The boss was happy with our sales, and I was more than happy with the money I was paid.

He asked me if I wanted to take a van out the next day [Sunday]

I arrived at the yard at 12 o'clock and picked up my van, after about an hour of touring the streets another ice cream van pulled up behind me.' What do you think you are doing? the man from the other van asked me, he sounded and looked very angry. The first and obvious thing that came to mind was perhaps not the best thing to say, so, I just said Why. This is my patch, now bugger off. He then got in his van and overtook me. Not knowing the protocol, and seeing how angry he was, I thought it was best to go to another estate. Back at the yard my boss told me I could go wherever I liked, as there were no rules, he just said make sure you are in front of any other vans.

After my first weekend, my commission for selling the ice cream was more than I got for a week as an apprentice joiner. Also, with Pat helping me, we could spend the weekend together, and we were saving a lot of money for our wedding.

Each weekend I would try to improve my sales, first I thought my Pied Piper jingle wasn't very loud, and even though I had sold my guitar, I still had my amplifier, so I connected the speaker to the sound box in my van. Now you were left in no doubt I was on my way. The second thing I tried was, instead of putting 2 gallons of water to a gallon of cream I started to add a little more water, eventually, I was putting in 3 gallons of water, without any complaints from my customers, this boosted my commission by 25%.

One of my best weekends was when my boss sent me to Oulton Park Race Track. As soon as I pulled up on the grass I had a queue of customers, and it was like this for the rest of the day. Pat didn't come with me on this trip, but was amazed at the amount of money I made on that weekend.

Now with the extra money we were earning we decided to get engaged.

The photo below was taken in my parents' flat on the 2nd of November 1968, the day we got engaged.

This photo was also taken in the living room of our flat. My mum had won the camera in a competition that was on the back of a Kellogg's cornflakes packet. In 1968 most pop bands were getting more outrageous with their look, but I was happy to hang on to my 1964/65 look. I was definitely more of a Mod, rather than the leather clad Rockers.

Up to now my teenage years had been fantastic, fashion, fabulous music, learning to play the guitar and playing in a rock band, passing my driving test, spending nights with lots of new friends down the British Legion Club, going to football matches and even traveling around the country to different football grounds watching them play, and of course meeting Pat. All of this happened in just 5 years from 1963 to 1967.

Now, after getting engaged in 1968 all we were doing was working and saving. I would go down to Pats house after work and if the weather was kind we would go on long walks. If it was raining, we would sit in Pats kitchen, and with my tape recorder we would play all the music that we loved. We both had our favourites, mine, of course, was The Beatles, even though Pat liked them, her favourite group was Gerry and the Pacemakers, but there were literally hundreds of songs from that time that we both loved and would play on those rainy winter nights.

We had worked out that we would need at least a thousand pounds for our wedding and the deposit for our new home. It was definitely a difficult time for both of us, we had been used to going out and enjoying ourselves.

There were times, like everyone, we would have our disagreements. I suppose you could put most of that down to boredom. Some of the highlights of this time would be if Pats or my parents went out for the night and we could sit in the living room, just the two of us watching TV, or if one of Pats relatives asked us to baby sit.

Regardless of how much importance we put on saving as much money as we could, we decided in the summer of 1969 we would try to have a holiday. The problem was we didn't have a car.

I remember standing outside Pats house talking to her dad [Harry] he had just had a new car, it was a Simca 1300. I had just gone outside to admire his car, when the conversation turned to me saying how we would like to go on holiday but, now without a car I couldn't see how we could manage it. Without a seconds thought he said that if I hired a cheap little car for two weeks then he would use that for going to work and then we could borrow his new car for our holiday. At first, I said no, after all, he had only had this new car for a few hours, and now he was saying we could use it for our holiday, but he insisted that's what we should do. So, you can see our relationship had come on a good way from our first meeting when he told me to "swine off" to now offering to lend us his new car.

This holiday would have to be done on a budget. I thought somewhere in North Wales would be good. We decided on Barmouth, as it was only 100 miles from home, and because I had been there a few times with my parents I knew it quite well. To keep costs down we thought that if we slept in the car for one night and then the following night book a Bed and Breakfast, that way we could at least have a bath or shower every other night.

The first day we spent walking around the town, one thing I was starting to realise about Pat, and that was, shops are like a magnet to her, it was difficult to walk past a shop without hearing the words, let's go in and have a look around. After our shopping expedition we got in the car and found a big lay-by, we had moved up in the world and instead of the primus stove we now had a small Calor-gas stove. Pat managed to make some good roadside meals. Our first night spent on that lay-by was a bad move, with cars and wagons driving past shining their headlights into the car.

The next morning, we went to Portmeirion and the Italian Village, it had been built in the mid 1920s to copy a typical Italian village, this was a beautiful place, and back then we never dreamed that one day we would or could ever travel abroad. So, to visit this village was as close as we thought we would get to seeing what it must be like to be in Italy. It is set on a hillside overlooking the estuary, and walking around the Italian streets and gardens on a very sunny day was about as far away from the walks we would do around our council estate on a wet winter's night.

At about the same time as we visited the Italian village, a television series was made there. It became very popular, and had a cult following, it was called The Prisoner. I watched it on the telly only because we had been there, but it was a weird series and made no sense to me.

After we left the Italian village, we made our way to a place called Dyffryn Ardudwy, it was somewhere I had been to with my parents. I remembered it had a fantastic beach and   sand dunes. To get to the beach we had to travel down a long country lane and just by the start of the dunes there was a flat sandy area that was used as a car park. Because it was so hot, the first thing we did was walk through the dunes and went into the sea, just to cool down, it's got to be one of the best beaches you will find anywhere. Back at the car we could see in the distance a caravan site. I thought, instead of finding a B&B for the night, we spend the night on this car park and use the caravan sites toilets and washing facilities.

Once it started to go dark the car park emptied, and it was just us left, we settled down for the night. It was a clear sky and the Moon was very bright. History was being made that night, the Americans had sent up a manned spacecraft and they had just successfully landed on this bright shining ball in the sky. We were all alone on this car park, it was very quiet and it felt a bit eerie, this, in a funny way made it feel even more special, just the two of us looking up at the

Moon and wondering what it must be like for those Astronauts to be the first to walk on the Moon.

Funny how sometimes things work out for the best.

The following day I remembered a place called Nefyn, that I had been to a few years earlier with my parents, it had a beautiful bay, with about 4 whitewashed fishermen's cottages sitting on the edge of the beach. You could only get to it by going down a very steep winding road, but I thought it would be a nice place to take Pat. We arrived, and went down to the beach.

Music was so important to both of us, and along with the pop music we were now getting from the Beeb, there were also the pirate radio stations, like Radio Caroline that we could tune into. Radio Caroline was a ship that was anchored about 10 miles out to sea, this allowed them to broadcast pop music 24 hours a day 7 days a week, without being tied down to any rules or regulations set out by the government. So, to play all this music we had taken my dad's portable radio with us. After about an hour the battery in the radio ran out, we went to a small electrical shop on the High Street to get a new one. We got talking to the lady in the shop and she asked us if we had seen any of the Moon landing, [this was big news back in 1969]. When I explained to her that we were on holiday, and we hadn't managed to see any of it. I did mention to her that we had been looking up at the Moon the night before, and wondering what it must be like to be the first man to walk on the Moon. She started to tell us all about how the landing had gone, then she said, they would be showing it on the telly most of the day. The next thing she did shocked us both, she went into the back of the shop and came back with a key. She just said, this is the key to my house, it's just up the Highstreet, you can go and watch it for yourselves. We couldn't believe it, this lady who had only known us for a few minutes, was now giving us the key to her house. She said no one will be in, but I don't want you to miss it, she did say her son may be in soon, and if he did, just explain to him why we were there. So off we went to this little terraced house and let ourselves in, turned on the telly and settled down to watch it. After about half an hour we heard the front door open, and in walked her teenage son. The look on this young lad's face was a picture, seeing us two sitting in his living room watching his television. I quickly explained it to him and I don't remember him saying much, he just sat down and watched it with us.

After about two hours it was over, so we gave him back the key, and asked him to thank his mum very much. We did call in the shop on the way back to the car, but she wasn't there. I so regret not asking her name, or remembering her address, so we could have sent a thank you letter.

We started to head back to the car park by the sand dunes at Dyffryn, as I thought it was a perfect spot, especially with the facilities provided by the caravan site. This is where I started to learn that a certain look from Pat, without any words, were enough to let me know that, perhaps, this wasn't my best idea, she wouldn't shake her head or pull a disgruntled face, it was quite simply the eyes 👀. The eyes told me that she wasn't going to spend a third night sleeping in the car. So, we found a house that was advertising Bed and Breakfast. When we booked the room, it was cheaper to have one double room rather than two singles.

You may remember our last holiday, where we had to have two caravans, because, Pat's mum didn't think it was right for two teenage boys to share a caravan with the girls, also Pat and Viv were 100% in agreement with her mum. Well things hadn't changed on that moral front. The most

160

exciting thing for Pat at this B&B was having a bath, for me it was a full English breakfast, but we were both looking forward to sleeping in a proper bed. This was the first time either of us had stayed in a B&B, and the sleeping arrangement was also a first, but like me at the time, don't get too excited. There were 4 pillows on the bed, I had two, Pat had one and the 4th was put down the middle of the bed between us!!

I found a letter that my mum had saved, it was a letter I sent to them from this holiday, it mentioned how much we had paid for the B&B, it was £2-10/- [£2- 50p in today's money] the mistake I made was saying it was a double room. Saying we had a double room must have shocked my mum. She took the letter down to Pats mum and asked her what she thought about us sharing a room. Pat's mum just said, who don't you trust, my daughter or your son?

Pat sitting on a lay-by eating her lunch, this was how we had most of our meals on that holiday. I have to say all the cooking credit must go to Pat; I was just the dish washer.

The beautiful beach at Dyffryn Ardudwy, by the sand dunes where we spent quite a few nights sleeping in the car.

We had a brilliant holiday without breaking the Bank.

By the time we got back from this holiday, I was reaching the end of my 5-year indentured apprenticeship. Up to now being an apprentice gave me a little protection against the nasty site agent, that from my very first day, had tried to make my life awkward, basically, because he was a bully. He would bully others on the site's we worked on too, but I would stand up to him, and give as good as I got. He had it in for me because I wouldn't give in to his bullying.

The last week of my apprenticeship I was working on a site on Victoria Rd, Fenton. We were building a small block of units, for two shops. I knew my future wouldn't be with J. W. Walton. I thought that as soon as my apprenticeship ended, the nasty site agent would find a reason to sack me, and I wasn't going to give him that satisfaction. So, on that last week of my apprenticeship, I handed in my notice. But obviously, with all the plans Pat and me had with saving for our wedding and the deposit for our first home together, I would need to get a job, and quick.

163

I hadn't told Pat or my parents that I would be out of work by Friday. I got the local paper, and started to look for a job, if I spotted something I would nip off the building site to the phone box and ring them. Each time they would have my information, telling me they would let me know. By Friday I was getting desperate. I rang for two jobs but got the same answer as the rest. At the end of the day, I made my way home, jobless. I was dreading telling my parents what I had done, but even worse, telling Pat.

I sat having my evening meal, wondering how I was going to break the news to them. At about 6-30 there was a knock on the door, my mum went down to answer it. A man was asking to see Mr Williams, my mum invited him in and introduced him to my dad. He said his name was Brian from Henry Boots, my dad looked puzzled, Brian then said, the office had passed on this address to him, as someone had rung, enquiring about the maintenance joiner's job. I quite sheepishly said that it was me that had rang. We sat down at the table, and Brian explained what the job involved. It was doing the final checks on the houses on a very big council estate before the new tenants moved in. This sounded brilliant, but even better, my wages when I left my old job was £19 a week, he was now offering me £27. The building site was in Crewe, which was about 10 miles from home, but they put a free bus on each morning from our town centre. So, my days of traveling to work on the back of a wagon were over.

Monday morning, at 7-30 outside Burtons clothes shop in Tunstall was the pickup point. After Brian had gone, I explained it all to my parents. Then I started to get a bit worried about the number of tools I had. Joiners would have a big tool box that would be kept in one of the site huts. They would also have a canvas bag in which they would put whatever tools were needed for the day. Up to now, a tool bag was all I had. I did have quite a lot of tools, but I thought a few more were needed for a job like this. My dad suggested we went to Hanley [the main shopping centre] The first place we went, was to Rosina Wards, this was the second-hand shop I had got my guitar from. We did find some joiners tools, but as we were looking through all the piles of mixed-up things that made this shop special, I not only found tools, but this magical shop came to my rescue. A big black joiner's box was hiding among the treasures that this shop was full of, not only a tool box but a good selection of tools inside it too. [54 years on, and I still have that tool box]

Monday morning, with all my tools to carry, my dad offered to give me a lift to the pick-up place by Burtons shop. He dropped me off at 7 o'clock to give himself time to get to work. I stood there for about 15 minutes before some other men started to arrive. Then they started to separate into different groups. The first bus to arrive had the name "Seddon" on the front, and a group of men got on it, a few minutes later a second bus pulled up, with the name "Elsby" on the front. Then, at last my bus arrived, with the name "Henry Boot" on it, I lugged my tool box on and sat down. I can't remember ever going to Crewe before, but was happy in the knowledge that the driver knew the way. Eventually the bus pulled onto the building site, so my life as a joiner [not the apprentice anymore] was about to start. I asked where the site agents office was, and was directed to a long site hut. I knocked on the door, and went in, introducing myself, the site agent looked a bit puzzled, and said, the only joiner starting that day was a shuttering joiner. So, I explained that I had been given the job as the maintenance joiner. Well, he said, I don't know what you are going to do your maintenance on, as we are only just putting the footings in. I told him that a man

165

named Brian, from Henry Boot had called at my house on Friday night, offering me a maintenance job, on a council estate, that they were building in Crewe. This site agent said they were building a factory, not council houses, also this site was in Middlewich not Crewe. Apparently, I had got on the wrong Henry Boot bus. He did offer me a job as a shuttering joiner, but this isn't what I wanted, after he realised, I wasn't going to accept his offer, he said he would ring the Crewe site and let me speak to them. Luckily it was Brian who took the call. He just said wait there, I will come and pick you up. So better late than never I arrived in Crewe. Thankfully, Brian found it quite funny, he said, I could tell by our conversation on Friday night that you wanted the job. So, I was surprised when you didn't turn up this morning.

This job turned out to be brilliant, I was given a list each morning from the clerk of the works, who was employed by the council. He would go into the houses the day before and make a list of jobs that needed to be done. He was probably in his 50s, and regardless of the weather, he wore a long coat and trilby hat, and came to work on a push bike. I got on with him very well. My job was a bit like being self-employed, as I didn't answer to anyone other than the clerk of the council. If I did the jobs to his satisfaction then all was good.

The houses were very big, I was impressed with the quality of them, they had fitted kitchens, this was very unusual for the time, they also had central heating, almost unheard of back then. It was the end of August 1969 when I started on the site, by the time winter arrived, it would be freezing, but I soon worked out that if I put a fuse into the electric box, I could get the central heating working. So, with my flask of tea, sandwiches, and snacks, it was like home from home, in fact it was better than home, as we didn't have central heating back then.

Once the houses were passed by the clerk, the council would hand over the keys to the new tenant, and as far as I was concerned, they were very lucky tenants. After they had been occupied for six months, the clerk would do a final inspection, and give me a list of new jobs. Working in a house that people were now living in could throw up some strange situations. One job I had was to move a wardrobe, to replace some skirting board. Behind this wardrobe was about ten wads of money, rolled up with an elastic band around each one. I wasn't sure whether I should mention it to the lady of the house, as I thought, if I did, I could have a very disgruntled husband telling me off for giving away his hiding place. I came across some sights on this final maintenance, but I did get lots of tea and biscuits.

Below is the card that was put in my wage packet on the final day of my apprenticeship. After 5 years, there was no presentation to recognise my achievement, no fancy scroll, it was just this card about the size of a credit card, put in with my £19 final wages.

This is to Certify that

Melvyn John Williams

has satisfactorily completed an indentured apprenticeship in the Building Industry

as a

Joiner

For the North Staffs. Local Joint Apprenticeship Committee for the Building Industry.

E. Seddon Signing Representative

I'm not sure who took this photo of me, but it was taken in 1968 in the workshop at the college that I had to attend one day a week throughout my apprenticeship. I really didn't like these college days. First, I had a five-mile bus journey and had to be there by 9 o'clock, then at 5 o'clock the day class ended and we had to hang around the college until 7 o'clock when the 2-hour night class started. By the time I got home it would be about 10 pm, so it ended up being a 14-hour day, and I would only be paid for 8 hours.

Pat was obviously happy with my new job, as we could now save more money for our big day. A date had been set for March the 14th 1970, this would be 10 days after Pats 19th birthday.

We had been saving hard, and just about managed to save the £1,000 that we thought we needed for our wedding and deposit on our new home. The most important thing, was getting the building society to agree a mortgage. We had saved with the Halifax, so we went to them first. One thing they pointed out to us, was, as we were both under 21, we would need Guarantor's. Thankfully both Pats dad and my dad agreed to do this for us. We put in our application; all we could do now was wait for the building society to make its decision. Every day I hoped the letter from them would arrive in the post. It was 10 long days before the postman delivered a letter to Mr M Williams and Miss P Cartwright. It was Saturday morning, I sat on the step by our front door just looking at this letter, I was afraid to open it. When eventually I did, it was just 3 lines, a very short letter for something so important to us, but it was 3 lines of good news. So, now we could officially go house hunting.

A new, small estate, of semi-detached houses were being built, just off Furlong Road. This was just at the back of Pats grandparent's house. They were in our price range of £3,000. The builder wanted £25 deposit to secure one of the houses, it was also close to both our parent's, and we obviously knew the area, so, we paid the £25. It only took Pat about a week to decide she didn't want to live here, she had been talking to her uncle, and he said, they were being built on a shoredruck, now I'm sure a lot won't know this word, but it's a potteries slang word, for land-fill, created by pottery manufacturers. It's basically all the broken cups and plates that they would dump over the years, then cover over with a thin layer of soil.

We started to look again, and in the local paper we found a Bungalow in a place called Whitehill. We had never thought of buying a Bungalow and hadn't a clue where Whitehill was. We rang the estate agent and found out it was near to Kidsgrove, now, we had heard of that. So off we went to view it, it was dark when we got there. The Bungalow was about 18 months old, and the price was £2,950, it seemed nice, so we decided this was the one.

13 Brieryhurst road was our new, and first home.

It had quite a steep drive, this would get us in trouble on frosty or snowy days. As it was dark when we first went to view it, we didn't go and look at the back garden, so, when we eventually saw it in daylight, we were more than happy. It was 66ft long with lovely views, and in the distance, we could see Mow Cop Castle. This was a folly built by Randle Wilbraham in 1754, he was the Lord of the Manor at the time. It stands on a rocky outcrop and is the highest point in Stoke-on-Trent. The views from there are breathtaking, looking over Cheshire, you can see Manchester, Liverpool, and the Welsh Hills, and in World War Two, the pilots would use Mow Cop Castle as a reference to guide them home.

Anyway, back to our own little castle, we had two good sized bedrooms, the bathroom was small as was the kitchen, but the Living room was a good size, but it had this horrendous royal blue carpet, that would show everything up on it. Pat would hoover that bloody carpet two or three times a day, but we couldn't wear it out or afford to replace it. Before we moved in, we decided to do some decorating and tile part of the kitchen. Tiles were very cheap back then, so, the "Royal" we, chose the tiles. Tiling wasn't something I had done before, but it couldn't be that hard, could it? So, I started to put the tiles on, and I have to say, they were looking good. It was team work, I stuck them on and Pat did the grouting.

We were very proud of our handy work; Pats uncle Fred came to look at our new home. He worked at a fireplace manufacturer. We proudly showed him our tiling, he very matter of fact, pointed out that I had put most of them on upside down. They were called chicken tiles, and if you looked very closely at the pattern, you could just make out a chicken's head intertwined in the design, but it was too late to change them, so some of the chickens had to spend the rest of their life upside down!!

We had some strange ideas in the 1970s, along with our inherited blue carpet we matched that with a pair of orange curtains. Also, the in-thing to do back then was to paper the ceiling [this was before artex.] with two kitchen chairs and the paper pasted, we started to work our way across the room, Pat was holding the roll of paper while I fixed it to the ceiling, we got to the other side of the room, only to find the paper had peeled off and was following us.

All I can say is, thank goodness that idea has never made a comeback.

THE BUILD UP TO OUR BIG DAY

AND HONEYMOON

First, we had to do the normal things, like, go and have tea and biscuits with the Vicar, and book the reception venue. Then I went with David, my best man, to a shop in Town, and instead of just picking up a suit off the peg, a man with a tape measure around his neck started to show us different pieces of material, a grey pinstripe was suggested by the man, and we thought, why not!! He even talked us into having a waist coat. Then the tape measure was whipped from around his neck, and measurements were taken, David went first and one of these measurements took him a bit by surprise and he gave out a little squeak, and his head spun round with a look of shock on his face, but apparently, it's a very important measurement.

One of the things we paid for was having the invitations printed. About two weeks before our wedding we got them back from the printers, I was very impressed, they looked good. We showed them to our parents and I don't know why, but this piece of card sort of made it official. Then Pat noticed a problem, our wedding was at 2 o'clock, but the invitations say 2-30. There was no time to have them reprinted, so, we went to see the Vicar, and thankfully he agreed we could get married 30 minutes later than planned.

Now I promise you, this wasn't my idea.

A few weeks before our wedding, Pat had made a unanimous decision that we should have Dancing lessons ●● Along with two friends, we started our lessons. You may be familiar with the saying, he's got two left feet, well this was a good way to describe my attempt at dancing, but Pat insisted that practice makes perfect, I did point out to her that the word perfect would be stretching it a bit, but we stuck at it. The dance studio was above the local cinema. The two professional teachers were doing their best with me. They were man and wife; he had the short back and sides Brylcreem hair style and his wife had a blond beehive. In one of the breaks, I got talking to them, and because they knew I was a joiner, they asked me if I could make some tables for the dance studio. There were rows of chairs around the dance floor, but nothing for people to put their drinks on. Just finding the time to make these tables was the problem, but I politely said I would try to sort something out.

The 14th of March 1970 was a cold, but sunny day.

Pat arrived at the church 10 minutes late, as is the tradition, but she looked beautiful. The ceremony went well, I think the hardest bit was outside, having the photos taken and being asked to constantly smile for 30 minutes in the cold.

The reception was just a short drive down the road from the Church, at the Talisman pub. It was a buffet [not many had sit-down meals back then]. After we had spent time talking to our guests and the obligatory cutting the cake, Pat made the short trip across the road to go to see her grandad, who a few years earlier had had a stroke and was house bound. Pat thought the world of her grandad, and wanted to show him her wedding dress and to spend a little time with him. It was a very emotional visit for both of them.

The Talisman had also been booked for the evening, as quite a few people had travelled from Nottingham, and it was a nice way for everyone to catch up with relatives who hadn't seen each other for a while. We missed this, as we were off to Stoke railway station to start our 24-hour honeymoon in London. The size of the suitcase that we

174

took for our overnight stay was as big as most people would take for a week. This was something that over the next 50+ years I would have to get used to. It could rain, it could snow, it could be hot, but you won't catch Pat out 👀. We arrived at Euston station about 7pm, and we were about to experience our very first ride in a Taxi. I had seen it on the telly and films, you just put up your arm, and like magic a black cab would pull up, and wow, to my amazement it worked. Where to Guv, he said. [well, probably not] but let's imagine that's what he said for the sake of a bit of artistic license. The Taxi took us to the Royal Hotel, I know, it sounds posh, but don't be fooled. The ride took about 10 minutes, and we checked in and given the key to our room.

We managed to get something to eat, but the bright lights of London were not for us, we were knackered.

Imagine a room on the 5th floor that had a bed and just a small table with a window, with no curtains or blinds. The room was about 10ft x 8ft, but none of this mattered to me. I had thought about this first night as a married couple so many times it was going to be so romantic!!

Pat said that after the long day we had had, she wanted a nice soak in a bath, there was no en-suite bathroom. The only bathroom was down the hall, and was shared with the other rooms. She came back after what seemed forever, and it was my turn to go and freshen up. On my way back to our room, I thought, well at least I won't have a pillar down the middle of the bed this time. I opened our bedroom door, only to be met with a gentle serenade of zzzzzzz coming from Pat - not quite as planned, so I climbed in bed and closed my eyes. I remember the room was so hot, and the neon lights of London were flashing through our bedroom window all bloody night.

The next morning, we had to walk down the corridor and take our turn for the bathroom, although, thankfully, the breakfast was good, with lots to choose from.

When Pats uncle had found out we were going to London, he told us that his son was living down there studying at one of the Universities. So, he arranged for us to meet up with him and his wife on the Sunday morning.

As we walked out of our hotel, they were waiting for us. Pat's cousin asked where we would like to go. We hadn't really planned anything, so we suggested the obvious things like Buckingham Palace, Downing Street, and we wanted to see Big Ben. Within minutes of walking down the road we were taken down some steps and onto the underground. We did this about 4 times, each time we got off the train, and back up to the street, one of the landmarks that we had asked to see would be there in front of us. We were so impressed with our guides, not only for taking us to all these places, but also their knowledge of the history.

One final surprise before it was time to head home, Pats uncle had sent his son some money down, so that he could take us to a posh restaurant. We had a wonderful day, then it was back to Euston station and on the train home.

On the train back to Stoke we had got less than a £1 between us, so it was with a sigh of relief when we got off the train to see my mum and dad had decided to pick us up. We eventually got home around 11 pm.

We woke up on Monday morning, with the rest of the week off work as part of our honeymoon. After managing to save a thousand pounds for our wedding we were now down to our last pound. Fortunately, we had paid our mortgage and utility bills, and had a few tins of food in the cupboard. I decided to go and see the couple who ran the dance studio to see if they still wanted me to make the tables. Thank goodness the answer was, yes please. The next question was, would they pay for the materials, and then pay for the labour after I had made them. Again, they were happy to do that, so, our spare bedroom became our workshop, with Pat as my apprentice we set about making 8 tables.

Cornflakes, beans on toast and cups of tea kept us going. Pat's mum invited us twice to go to them for a meal, we were too proud to tell anyone we were broke, but those two meals were more welcome than they could ever imagine.

By Thursday all the tables were made and delivered, and we got paid. The first thing we did was to go food shopping.

This was our honeymoon week.

This next little story wasn't in our honeymoon week, but was part of our early married life.

Pat would cook some good meals, but every now and then she would turn to the easy option. Some of you will know the Frey Bentos pies in a tin. Pat put the pie in the oven and with a few chips and peas it seemed a good meal. About 20 minutes later we heard what sounded like a bomb going off. Apparently, you should take the lid off the tin first. Our new oven looked like a tangled piece of metal after the pie had exploded. Fortunately, Pats uncle [the one who paid for our meal in London] worked for the gas board, and managed to get it repaired.

Pat and her dad [Harry] arriving at the church

At the reception, just before we left for London

Pat's grandad, who she thought the world of, and made a
special trip to see him halfway through the reception.

A LESSON LEARNED

I don't know if any of you did this, we had a tin that was divided into different sections, and each week we would put money in each section. One would be for the mortgage, one for the gas bill, and so on. When the bill was due, we would simply take the money and go to the building society or the Gas board shop in town, pay the bill and get it stamped. One of the things we did was to take out an insurance policy, this was something both our parents did, I think it was with the Wesleyan General. You paid so much a month, then after 10 years, if you hadn't made a claim, you got your money back with a little interest on top. Tony was our insurance man, who would call at our house to collect the money. we had known him for years; from the time he would call at our parents' house. He was a really nice man who would always ask how we were, and would remember everyone's name.

Now we were married, I was starting to feel like my parents, each Saturday we would go into town and do the shopping. This, as a young boy, I hated, being dragged around the shops, but now I had no choice. As far as Pat was concerned it was the highlight of the week, almost every shop was worth a look 👀

Up to now we had the basics in our new home, but one thing that Pat wanted was a wardrobe for our bedroom. We did have one wardrobe that had been given to us, but it had seen better days, and the previous owner had decided to paint it white, it looked so bad Pat wouldn't have it in our bedroom, it was relegated to the spare room. So, on one of our Saturday shopping trips, Pat grabbed my arm and pulled me back to look in the window of a furniture shop, look, she said, look at what? Look at that wardrobe, let's go in, I just want to see how much it is. As we stood looking at it, one of the sales-staff came over to us, but I quickly told him we were only looking, but that wasn't going to stop him. He told us of this offer that they had, basically, if you paid a small deposit, then we could pay off the balance over 3 months with no interest to pay. That's ok mate, I said, we are just looking. We walked out of that shop after paying just a small deposit on the double wardrobe with a mirror down the middle, a double man's wardrobe, a dressing table, a set of draws and even a stool for the dressing table. We had to use some of the money from our bills tin to pay this deposit, but we were confident that we had a month to replace it. Our bedroom, now, looked very posh, and by the end of the month we had replaced all the money, apart from our insurance payment. The day arrived when Tony was due to collect his money, he would normally arrive about 7 o'clock. Tony was like a friend, and we didn't know what to tell him, so, we went into our back garden at the time he was due to call. Both of us stood like statues with our backs to the wall, we could hear him knocking on our door. It went quiet and we both breathed a sigh of relief, then Tony came round the back to see us standing there. That has got to be one of the most embarrassing things we have ever done. We had to come clean and explain, he was very understanding, and said he would mark us down as being out. That was a lesson learned for us, don't have what you can't afford. This was 1971. It was in 2014 that I was shopping in Tesco when I saw Tony, he was well into his 70s, but like all good salesmen he remembered me by name, and asked how Pat was.

OUR FIRST TELEVISION

One other thing that springs to mind in those early days, was that Stoke City were to be on the telly on Saturday afternoon in a memorable cup game. It wasn't like today, when the telly is full of football matches. If your team was on the telly in the early 70s it was a special occasion.

We were doing our normal shopping in Tunstall. Up to now we hadn't got a television, we just couldn't afford one. As we walked past the electrical shop, I could see they were advertising televisions, you didn't have to buy them outright, or even pay a deposit, all you had to do was have a slot meter that was fixed to the back of the telly. For a change, it was me wanting to go into the shop. I said to the salesman that if he could deliver and install it by 3 o'clock in time for the football match, then we would have it.

True to his word, it was delivered and installed in time for the game. I put my 2 shillings, [10p] into the slot meter and watched the game, Stoke won, beating Chelsea 2-1 in the League Cup final at Wembley.

The television was never yours; it was like renting it, they would come round each month to empty the meter. It was a daft idea, the times we would be halfway through watching a programme and it would just go off, so you had to search round to find 10p to put in the slot, or even go next door asking if they had 10p

We didn't have this telly for long!!

BACK TO 4 WHEELS, UNWELCOME ENCOUNTERS WITH THE LAW, AND A FEW OTHER THINGS.

Even though we were enjoying living in a semi-rural area, we found it difficult without a car. Harry mentioned he had seen a van for sale at a garage that he passed on his way home from work, and offered to take me to look at it. We were told it belonged to one of the mechanics, I don't know if this was supposed to reassure me that it was in good order. The price was £95, so we became the proud owner of a very bright yellow van.

I had worked for Henry Boot for the last eighteen months as the maintenance joiner, and I had enjoyed every minute, but the site was coming to an end. All the houses were now built, the only thing left to do was the final maintenance. Along with a plasterer a decorator, plumber a labourer and me as the joiner, we were the only people left on the site. The building firm stopped running the free bus to the site, instead, they paid me a travelling allowance, so getting the van came at just the right time. There was only me and the labourer that travelled from Stoke to the site in Crewe, the others lived locally.

Levison [Lev] the labourer had become a good friend of mine over the last 18 months, he lived in Smallthorne, close to the place that my dad was born, and he hadn't got any transport. To help him keep his job, even if it was only for the next few weeks, I offered to give him a lift each morning. Lev gave me his travel allowance to help with the petrol, the only problem was that he lived 4 miles in the opposite direction from the site.

Since having my bright yellow van, it had started to attract attention, and I would get pulled over by the police. One morning I set out to pick up Lev, and within a mile, I was pulled over, the policeman was very polite, and just asked me to take my insurance and licence to the police station in the next 3 days. This same morning, I was stopped twice more before I got to work. I tried to explain that I had already been stopped, but it made no difference, so, with three tickets I went down the police station. The man

184

behind the counter found it quite funny, and over the next few weeks me and the policeman at the station were on first name terms.

Lev was due to get married and invited us to the wedding. I asked him if they would be having a honeymoon, he said his wife-to-be wanted to go to Blackpool, but he didn't think it would be possible as they hadn't got any way of getting there. I had a word with Pat, and we thought that if we had a night in a B&B at Lytham St Annes, we could drop them off in Blackpool. After the wedding, Lev and his Bride climbed into the back of my van, and we set off on the 80-mile trip. I've got to say there was a lot of laughing on that journey, as Lev and his wife rolled about in the back of the van. They didn't want or ask for much, but they said they had a brilliant 24 hours honeymoon in Blackpool.

It was getting close to Christmas 1970, and all we had to do on the building site was to dismantle all the site huts and tidy up. It proved to be a very good opportunity for me and my van, I managed to rescue quite a few things that would just be dumped. I got a lot of timber that I was able to use to put a fence around our garden, there were bricks that I gave Harry to build a wall in his garden. I even managed to get some kitchen units, but my biggest prize wasn't from the houses we had built. Part of the site had had some prefab houses that had been built just after WW2. These houses were built as temporary accommodation after the war, but they had been so well built they lasted much longer than planned. Unfortunately, the prefabs on this site had to be demolished to make room for the new estate. In one of the sheds that we were now taking down, I found some small refrigerators that had been taken out of the old prefabs. I put one of these refrigerators in my van, Pat was so excited, I can't tell you how proud we were to say we had a fridge. It's hard to believe that these prefabs had refrigerators, but most houses up to the 1970s still only had a cold slab to help keep their food fresh.

Christmas day was on Friday, it was always good to have Christmas at or near to the weekend, that way it gave us a longer break. We only had Christmas day and Boxing day off, so when it fell close to the weekend we would have 4 days off. Thursday, we had our pay packet and a letter informing us that we would be made redundant the following Friday. It didn't come as a surprise to the 5 of us that were left on the site, but finding a job on a building site in the middle of winter was almost impossible.

On new years eve Pats parents had a family party. I got talking to Pats uncle, and said that I would be out of work the next day, he mentioned that he had a few jobs I could do at his house, this wasn't going to pay the mortgage, but anything was better than nothing.

Pats uncle Geoff was a nice man and had a wicked sense of humour, he had nicknames for everyone, for me it was Melvine. Even when he could see I was worried about being out of work, he just said, look Melvine I've got a few jobs you can do for me. I turned up at his house on Monday morning. Geoff worked at Rolls Royce on the night shift. The Rolls Royce factory was in Crewe, and not far from the building site that I had just left. He said that when he went to work that night he would ask if there were any jobs going. The following day he told me there were jobs available, and he gave me the phone number of the personnel office. I rang but they said there was nothing available. The next day Geoff said he had asked again, and there were jobs in the inspection department, so I rang again, this time they asked me to go for an interview. After explaining my situation, the personnel manager said, they don't like employing people from the building trade, as they thought that come spring, they would just go back out

186

on the building sites again. I tried to explain that wasn't the case, but he just said sorry we don't have any jobs.

Not one to give up, I rang again on Thursday, I said that I had been told about a job in the inspection department. I think by now they were getting fed up with me, the receptionist asked me to hang on while she went and spoke to someone. She came back and said that If I could be at the factory at 10 o'clock Friday morning the personnel manager would see me again. This time he tried to put me off by saying the job in the inspection department was a semi-skilled job, and he didn't think someone with a trade should take a job like this. By this time, I thought I had nothing to lose, so I just said, I have got a mortgage to pay, I'm looking for a job that has long term security, I don't care that its semi-skilled, I won't leave when the weather gets better, so, are you going to give me this job? At last, he said he would put me on a month's trial, and to report to the security office on Monday morning, and someone will take me to the inspection department.

That last story may sound a bit farfetched, but that's exactly how it happened, it took me from Monday to Friday to get the job, but with a mortgage to pay its surprising what you will do. It was explained to me that my month's trial would be on a reduced rate to start with. My job was to inspect engine parts for flaws. I had to put a small electric current through the part and coat it in a die that would show up any faults. It wasn't rocket science, and after my first week I was deemed good enough to work on my own. My starting pay was £25 a week, but now I was working on my own it went up to £32, so I was getting more than I was as a joiner. At first, I think I was more impressed with the canteen, the choice of food was like eating in a restaurant, and it was subsidised, so no more jam and ham butties for me.

A DREAM MADE INTO
A REALITY

At the age of 15, Pat was visiting her aunty, who had just had her second baby, and on this same day, the midwife called to check on mother and baby. It's at this time Pat decided that one day she could be a midwife. Although Pat was still at school, she started to make some enquiries, and, found out that you had to be 20 years old before you could apply to start your training.

Now in 1971 she put in her application, and went through the process of starting her midwifery training. I had no doubt she would make a brilliant midwife, but the problem was the travelling. To get to the Hospital, she, first had to get a bus to Tunstall, this was about a 4-mile trip, then get a second bus to Newcastle, again this was another 5-miles.

Then it was a walk of about a mile to the Hospital, and finally make her way to the basement of the Hospital to get changed into her uniform, before reporting for duty on the ward by 7-45 am.

If all this wasn't bad enough, we were terrible at waking up each morning, so, we had 3 alarm clocks that were positioned around the bedroom, all set at 5-minute intervals, and you had to get out of bed each time to switch them off. Then there came a time in her training that she was required to do night shifts. If the travelling to and from work wasn't bad enough, doing it at night, and then after a 9 and a half-hour shift, make that long journey home.

Pat had passed her driving test, first time, at the age of 18. Pats dad had insured his car so she could use it for her driving lessons, but he left it up to me to take her out, [wise man] so I became the driving instructor. I remember one time we were practicing hill starts, Pat was struggling with her clutch control, so I put a packet of 10 Park Drive cigarettes under the back wheel, so, if she didn't get it right, I would have 10 flattened cigarettes, thankfully, this was the inspiration needed, and she pulled off perfectly.

I digressed a little, obviously we couldn't afford two cars.

Up to this point my job at Rolls Royce was to start work at 7-55 and finish at 5 o'clock, but when Pat was asked to do her night shifts, I asked my supervisor if I could also do nights. I got on well with my boss, and he said all he could do was let me alternate, doing two weeks nights, then two weeks days. This was better than nothing.

The idea of us both doing nights at the same time, was, I could take Pat to work first, then make my way to Rolls Royce. We would set out at 8pm and get Pat to the Hospital by 8-30, this was half an hour before her shift started, but better than traveling by bus. Then I had a 14-mile journey to Crewe to start work at 9pm.

My night shift ended at 7-30am, then I made the trip to the Hospital to pick Pat up by 8am. We got back home around 8-30, and we were knackered, because, the day before our first night shift we hadn't managed to get any sleep, so we had been awake for 24 hours. We both sat on the side of the bed and flopped back, still fully clothed and our legs hanging over the side of the bed. We woke up in the same position at 7pm, so, we had one hour to get ready to start it all again. We found it hard enough trying to wake up, even with 3 alarm clocks. Now working nights, to give us a fighting chance of waking up on time, we invested in a 4th alarm clock, but this one I put in a tin box, to make even more noise.

189

THREE UNWELCOME CHANGES

In 1965 our government started to bring in changes to make it possible for us to join, what was then called, The Common Market, [eventually known as the European Union] the first thing they did was slowly introduce the Metric system of measurement. This wasn't a welcome move by most of the older generation, and even people like me, who had just left school. We had only known feet and inches, now they wanted us to use meters and centimetres, our gallon of petrol was now to be measured in litres. What a crafty move that was, when you saw the cost of petrol on the forecourt in litres, you first thought, oh that's not bad, until you multiplied it by 4.5 then you realised the crafty buggers had increased the price. They wanted me to say I was 1.77 Meters and not 5ft 10 inches tall. They wanted me to ask for things in kilograms. Well 58 years on, I'm still 5ft 10 inches, I still take my gallon container to get petrol from the garage for my mower, I still ask the Butcher for 2lbs of mince. So, until most of us from that generation are dead and gone, they will have to put up with us.

Another thing they did in 1973, was to introduce Value Added Tax, but they called it [VAT] they even implemented this Tax on the 1st of April, [all fool's day]

When we got married, someone had given us an old washing machine, it looked so bad, Pat wouldn't have it in our kitchen, it was kept in the spare room, so, when the washing had to be done, we had to push it from the spare room through the living room into the kitchen.

Pat had been telling me of this wonderful new automatic washing machine, she said, all you had to do was put your washing in before we went to work, press a button and when we got home your washing was all done.

I had been brought up in a time when washday was on a Monday. First you had to boil the water in the big wash tub, this had a lid on it and a tap at the bottom to drain off the water when finished. When you lifted the lid to put the clothes in, or add the soap powder, clouds of steam would fill the kitchen. The soap powder was usually Omo, Daz or Persil, and a little Robin Starch to give the clothes that crisp feel. Every now and then the lid was lifted and the wooden washing dolly was put in to swish the washing around by hand. When the washing was clean, it had to be dragged out and put in the Belfast sink to be rinsed in cold water. Then they would have to be rung out by hand, to get the excess water out. Finally, in the back yard there was the mangle, this had two wooden rollers that you fed the washing through by turning a big wheel, to get the rest of the water out. In good weather the clothes were hung out on the washing line. This was the risky bit, after all that hard work, you had to hope next door didn't light a fire and the soot from their chimney didn't fall on your clean washing. In winter time, the only option to get your clothes dry, was to hang them on the wooden clothes-horse around the coal fire. This, for me was the worst thing, as a young boy, if I had been playing outside in the snow, or on a freezing cold day, all I wanted to do was to sit by the fire to get warm, but if the clothes were draped around the fire, you not only couldn't get near the fire to get warm, you couldn't even see it, all you could see was the steam coming from the washing.

Saturday, the 31st of March 1973 was the last day before the new Value Added Tax [VAT] would become law and would be added to things like washing machines. The price of these items would increase by 8%.

So, now, Pats dream of owning one of the new automatic washing machines was something we had to do. We went into town to do our weekly shop, and went into the electrical shop, and ordered one. We had learned our lesson from the embarrassing time we used our bills money to pay for our bedroom furniture, this time we paid for it with our savings.

TIME FOR A CHANGE

We had been married for 3 years, when Pat started to fall out of love with our Bungalow. What she really wanted was a house, so we went looking around the area, we loved where we lived, and there were plenty of houses for sale, but none had got the open views from the back that we had got used to.

At about the same time, both our parents, after over 20 years of living on the council estate, decided they wanted to move. It was a total coincidence that they both made this decision at the same time. Pats parents found a nice 3 bedroomed Bungalow, in a place called Brown Lees, not far from where we were living.

My parents quite surprised me, when they said they had bought a plot of land, and were going to build their own house. It was very close to Bathpool Park, a beautiful nature reserve, that as a child I would spend many happy hours playing there with my mates. One Saturday morning we went to have a look at the plot of land they had bought. As we drove to the site we noticed a sign, advertising new houses for sale. There were 10 semi-detached houses at the end of a cul-de-sac, some were already built, but the end plot hadn't even got the footings in yet, but we fell in love with its position. It overlooked Bathpool Park and had a small wooded area at the end of the cul-de-sac. These houses had a large living room, a kitchen that was three times bigger than our Bungalow and 3 good sized bedrooms, it also had an integrated garage. The price was £6,500, more than double what we had paid for our Bungalow, so, we weren't sure if we could afford it. All we could do was to have our Bungalow valued, and we were amazed that in just 3 years, its value had gone from £2,950 to now, £5,000. we asked the building society, and they didn't see a problem. So, we put a deposit on this house that hadn't been built yet, and put our Bungalow on the market. It only took a week, and the first to view our Bungalow, decided they wanted it. What a dilemma, our new house was 4 months from completion, and we had to move out of our Bungalow. Pats parents came to our rescue, and said we could move in with them until our house was finished.

It was at this time, that Pat, in her midwifery training was required to spend 3 months living on the district that she was covering as a midwife. Along with 4 other students, she was expected to live and breathe midwifery, well at least from Monday to Friday. How it worked, was, Pat along with her 4-student midwife colleagues, would live in a house on the area they were covering. Each morning they would go out and visit their patients, teach ante natal classes etc.

Each night I would drive over to spend some time with Pat, and along with the other husband's and partners, we started to have quite a good social life. Over the 3 months that they had to all live together, we made some special friends. Sylv was the same age as Pat, and was engaged to Pete. When they eventually got married, Pete asked me to be his best man. Over the years we have had many holidays with them, also, both Pete and me enjoyed playing guitar, and we also started to play Tennis, [badly] but as time went on the guitar playing, and the tennis matches, became a big part of our social life. It's now 50 years since we first met Sylv and Pete, and today 13th of February 2023, is Pete's birthday, and we have just got back from having a meal with them to celebrate it.

194

At last, our new house was built, and with the help of Pats new midwifery mates and their partners, we moved in to 43 Shakespeare close. When the house was being built, Pats mum and dad had said that for a moving in present, they would pay for the living room carpet. So, it came as a shock to them when they realised how big the living room was, 26ft by 13ft, but thankfully they stuck to their word, and at last, Pat could say goodbye to the horrendous blue carpet we inherited with our first bungalow.

We had also said goodbye to our very bright yellow van. Before we sold it, we thought we should give it a wash, and clean the inside. Pat was doing the inside, and asked me what this round thing was hanging down below the dash board, it had a switch on the side. We had spent 3 freezing winters driving round in this van, and on the day, we sold it, was the day we realised this round thing was the heater!!

By 1974, I was still working at Rolls Royce. There was a job advertised on the factory notice board. It was assembling the dash boards on both Rolls Royce and Bentley cars. The hourly rate was a lot more than I was getting in the inspection department, as it was considered a skilled job. I put my application in, and got the job.

The inspection department that I had just left, after 4 happy years, was next to the section that finished the highly polished, and probably the most famous part of the Rolls Royce, it was officially called The Spirit of Ecstasy, but better known to most of us as The Flying Lady, and she took pride of place at the front of the bonnet, above the grill.

Anyone who was wealthy enough to buy a Rolls Royce, could have a tour of the factory, and one of the places that they would be taken on this tour, was, the Flying Lady section. From my inspection department, I could see, through the glass partition all the celebrities of the day, even Royalty, being shown how this iconic emblem was produced. No one was told in advance about who would be having the tour, and there was a very strict rule, we must not approach these celebs and not to ask for an autograph. It was always the same man that would do the demonstration, and if the celeb was someone I was interested in, after they had gone, I would go and ask what they were like.

Now in my new job, assembling the dash boards, I was given quite intense training. There was only 5 of us in this department. The first thing I was taught was to check that there were no flaws in this magnificent piece of wood, they were highly polished and had a join in the middle, and the wood veneer grain on the left must mirror perfectly the grain on the right. Our work bench had a soft felt material on it to prevent any damage to the wood, most of the clocks and dials were fixed from the back, but some had to be fixed on the front. I was constantly reminded, that one slip of my screw driver, could cost hundreds of pounds of damage. We weren't allowed to use power tools, only hand tools.

Now in this prestigious job, my little department was part of the celebrity's tour. We were told, don't speak to them, unless they speak to you first. out of the 5 of us, I was never the chosen one to give the demonstration, after all, I was the newbie, but I was close enough to hear the tour guide giving his speech, and most of the celebs were very nice and polite, and showed genuine interest in what we did.

I HADN'T GOT A CLUE

One of Pats friends from work was looking for a house, so Pat suggested that they look at one of the houses just 4 doors up from ours. Hilary was a student midwife too, and Stan, her husband, was a figure painter at Doulton's, we soon became friends, and would spend time together. I say this in the nicest possible way, but Stan and Hilary weren't your normal couple. They had some way-out ideas. One thing they did was to paint their hall, stairs, and landing in pillar box red, the stair-carpet was also dark red, and they even had red coloured light bulbs. Stan was very artistic, and he painted a wide stripe around the living room, that had all the colours of the rainbow in it, but regardless of these way-out ideas, we got on well with them.

Pat had now finished her 3 months stint, living in the house with the other students, and was back working on the maternity ward in the Hospital. She would never drive our little bright yellow van, but now we had a half decent car, she was happy to drive it. So, if I was on nights, I would get home from work, and, with the engine still running, Pat would get in the car and take herself off to work. as the saying goes, we were like ships that pass in the night.

One Monday, Pat had gone to work, and I was in the back garden, when Hilary came round the back with a big black bag, their washing machine was broken, and asked if she could use ours, after a while, and trying to work out what button to press, we got it going. We were sitting in the living room having a cup of tea, when the phone rang, [I know, we now had a phone] it was Pat, she just said she had had it confirmed, and she was pregnant. I hadn't got a clue, she hadn't said anything to me before, even though she was pretty sure herself.

We hadn't planned it, that's why, for me, it was a total shock. We had sort of talked about it, but there never seemed a time that was right, especially with Pat doing her midwifery training, but we were over the moon, it was the best news. Pat worked out that it would be close to Christmas when our baby was due,

Pats sister Ann, had got engaged to John, he was the son of the farmer, that Kath and Harry rented the land from for their caravan in Llanidloes, in mid Wales. John must have been very determined, because, as I mentioned before, he would have a 180 miles round trip to visit Ann. This would be my second time as best man. I think John's mates back in Wales didn't fancy the idea of making the best man's speech, and to be honest, things like this didn't bother me.

When they got married, Ann and John moved in with her parents.

In the summer of 1974, Kath, and Harry, spotted some bungalows that were being built, they were just up the road from us, and like when we bought our house, this bungalow was yet to be built. Ann and John decided to buy her parents bungalow. After the contracts were completed, which took months, Kath and Harry asked if they could move in with us, until their new bungalow was finished. I think the real reason was, that, Kath wanted to be near to Pat when the baby was born.

It was Sunday the 15th December, the 4 of us sat in the Livingroom playing cards, when, at around 6pm, Pat started to go into labour. She decided it was time to go to the Hospital.

When we arrived, we were taken down to the delivery rooms, there were 8 of them, and we were put in room 5.

Pat was quite calm, and kept reassuring me that everything was fine. It was like she was in her element, she said, she had seen hundreds of deliveries from the bottom half of the

198

bed, now she would be able to see what it was like from the top half. I, on the other hand, was totally out of my depth.

By 8 O'clock the following morning, nothing much seemed to be happening. I had been in the room most of the night with Pat, apart from nipping out to use the loo, or going to a room that the dads to-be could use if they wanted a cigarette. Also, throughout the night, Pat had been offered tea and toast, but I can only remember being offered one cup of tea. I went to the phone box to ring home, to give an update on the progress, well, there wasn't much progress, but I mentioned, I hadn't had anything to eat. Kath said she would send some sandwiches, and a flask of tea.

By the time I got back to the room, Gwyneth, who had been a student midwife at the same time as Pat, was in the room with her. Gwyneth and her husband Alan had become good friends, so it was nice to know she was there to do the delivery. At around 12 O'clock, things were starting to progress. We had been at the Hospital now for 18 hours, I sat at the top end of the bed, letting Pat and Gwyneth do their thing. At about 2-30, Gwyneth, said she would have to nip out of the room for a few minutes. When she came back, she had an Obstetrician with her, it was decided that the only way to get the baby out was with the help of forceps. I really wanted to be there for the delivery, but normally if a baby is delivered by forceps, they would ask the dad to go out of the room, but I was told I could stay, so long as I stayed at the top end of the bed. Even from there I could see the Obstetrician put the forceps into position and he started to pull, I thought, bloody hell, how can a new born baby stand that sort of thing. The Obstetrician was sweating, I was also sweating, Pat was squeezing my hand as tight as she could, and Gwyneth was standing there as cool as a cucumber. At 10 past 3pm on the 16th December 1974 Joanne Marie was born, weighing 7lbs 8oz. I must say, seeing your daughter being delivered by forceps after over 24 hours without sleep isn't to be recommended. But as the saying goes, Mother and Baby are both well. So, all was good.

After a phew phone calls, and spending some time with Pat and Joanne, I went home, just to get changed and to get something to eat.

I went back to the Hospital at 6 o'clock. It was amazing what a difference just 3 hours could make. Pat had been moved from the delivery rooms, and was now in a side room on the ward, with Joanne in a cot, at the side of the bed, and all was calm. It was just the 3 of us together for a short time, before everyone came to visit, it was the best feeling in the world.

Joanne, just 3 hours old

My mum on the left, with Pat's grandma holding Joanne and Pats mum on the right. They all arrived at 7 o'clock. Out of the hundreds of photos we have, this is one of my favourites.

This is a strange photo to include in the story of Joanne's birth. On the left is Alan and Gwyneth, and it was Gwyneth who was the midwife who helped to deliver Joanne, and she is one of the nicest people you could ever wish to know, Pat in the middle, and Sylv and Pete on the right, who I was best man at their wedding. Gwyneth, Sylv and Pat all trained to be midwives at the same time, and we all became good friends. The young lad kneeling is Alan and Gwyneth's son, and tucked up in the pram is 6 months old Joanne. We were on a caravan holiday with Pete and Sylv, near to Nefyn, and met up with Gwyneth and Alan for the day.

Alan was a good guitarist, and taught both Pete and me how to play Sloop John B, by the Beach Boys.

Pat and Joanne would spend the next 4 days at the maternity hospital. I suppose most new dads would get their wife/partner a nice bunch of flowers, to welcome them home, but, as a surprise, I went out and got something that we had been talking about for a while, and that was our first colour television. It wasn't brand new; it was one that the electric shop in town had rented out, and for whatever reason, it was returned to the shop, and they were selling it off at a fraction of the price of a new one.

I know, I should have got the flowers as well,

but I wasn't made of money. ☐

FROM THE PREVIOUS HAPPY STORY TO A VERY SAD ONE

Having Pat's mum and dad staying with us when Pat and Joanne came home from hospital was a big help. I was working two weeks nights then two weeks days, so it was ideal that Pat could have her mum with her, especially when I was working nights.

I got home one morning from my night shift and sat in the kitchen talking to Kath, she was telling me about a strange thing that had happened the night before. She said that she had got up in the night to go to the loo, and decided to go down stairs to make a cup of tea, when someone knocked on our door. [I don't think anyone would do this today], but she went to see who it was. There was a man standing at the door, and he was asking the way to Bathpool Park. This is a wild life park that is just down the road from our house, in fact, from our back living room window you can see the entrance to the park. She said he was talking fast, and seemed agitated. The directions were very simple, Kath just told him to go to the end of our road, turn right and that would take him to Bathpool Park. She said he didn't say thank you, he just got in his car and drove off. Neither of us could understand why anyone would want to go there at that time of night, especially in winter. It's a massive park with a big lake at the far end, and in the day time it was very popular with people just walking their dogs, or kids playing football, but at night it would be pitch black.

This happened late Friday night, and other than both of us thinking how strange it was, we didn't mention it again.

The following week I was coming home from work on Tuesday morning, and on the radio, they were talking about a young girl who had been kidnapped, but I was only half listening. When I got home, Pat said have you seen all the police cars down at the entrance to the park. As I looked out of the window, Kath said, she thought it was something to do with a 17-year-old girl who had been kidnapped a few days earlier. The first thing that I thought about was the man knocking on our door, so, I said to Kath that she should go down to the police and mention it to them. She didn't seem too keen, but asked me if I would go down to them. As I got to the entrance to the park, it was taped off, I told one of the policemen about the story of the man, and he immediately lifted the tape, and took me to two other men who were standing near the railway bridge, a few yards inside the park. They seemed very interested in my story and had my name and address, they said they would send someone to get a statement. I had no sooner walked back into the house when two policemen were knocking on the door. I explained to them that I was only the messenger, and it was Kath who they needed to talk to. They were in our house about an hour, asking the same questions over and over again. When they eventually went, I went to bed as I was on nights, but at around 2 o'clock in the afternoon, Pat woke me up and said the police are back, and they want to talk to you. They started off by asking me about the man knocking on the door, when I said I wasn't at home at the time, they wanted to know where I had been. I just told them I was at work, obviously they had all the information about who I worked for, and names of people they should talk to.

The following morning, I got in from work and went to bed, and the same thing happened, they got me out of bed and started asking more questions. By now I was starting to get a bit fed up, so I just said, have you rung Rolls Royce and asked them if I was at work, yes, they said. So, what more can I tell you? they just apologised.

It was quite a few weeks later, on the 7th of March 1975 that they eventually found the body of this poor girl, Lesley Whittle, she had been put down one of the drainage shafts, they found a mattress, a flask and torch on the shelf deep inside the shaft. She had been put in there alive by Donald Neilson, who was demanding £50,000 ransom for her release, but things hadn't gone to plan on the night the ransom money was to be paid. First the brother of Lesley Whittle had been instructed to deliver the ransom money, and to go to a phone box by the Post Office in Kidsgrove, where Neilson had left a message with instructions, but the brother took over half an hour to find these instructions, that had been put behind the black panel. Then he got lost on his way to Bathpool Park and it could have been him who knocked on our door that night, as our house was the last in the cul-de-sac and the Livingroom light was on, and it would seem a strange coincidence for anyone else to be asking for directions to the Park that late at night. The next thing to go wrong, was, even though Staffordshire police were involved in the covert operation, they hadn't told the local police station, which was just half a mile from the park. Two police officers in their panda car, unaware of the situation, had decided to park their car on the carpark that was right by the bridge, where the brother of Lesley had been instructed to take the ransom money. The combination of the brother being late, and the police car being parked by the bridge, was enough to scare Neilson off. The place where I first went down to the park to talk to the police, about the man knocking on our door, was just 20 feet from the shaft where they eventually found the body of Lesley.

As I write this, it is 48 years since that tragedy, and even now, when you walk past the sealed off drainage shaft, people still occasionally lay flowers.

It's a very sad story, of an horrendous crime, committed by this most evil man.

It was 10 months later, when two police officers were sitting in their panda car in a side road in Mansfield, Nottinghamshire, when they spotted a man carrying a holdall, walking along the road. As he passed their car, he turned his face away from the police car. One of the officers thought his actions looked suspicious, so they called him over to question him. The man said he was on his way home from work, but then produced a sawn-off shotgun from the holdall. He ordered the officers back into the car, one in the back seat and Neilson sat in the front passenger seat and pointed the gun at the driver. He instructed them to take him to a place called Rainworth, about 6 miles away. As they approached a road junction, the police man asked Nielson which way to go and as he looked up, the driver, seeing Nielson was distracted, started to swerve his car from left to right. This disorientated him and the policeman in the back took the opportunity to grab the gun, while the driver slammed on his brakes. The gun went off, luckily only grazing the policeman's hand. They came to a stop just outside a chip shop. Two very brave men who were in the queue outside the chip shop ran over to help, and overpowered Neilson. The two local men helped to drag him to some iron railings, and the policeman handcuffed him there, and called for backup.

In the subsequent investigation, Nielsons fingerprints were found to match one of those in the drain shaft. He eventually confessed to the kidnap.

Further enquiries also proved that Nielson had committed over 400 robberies and had murdered 4 other people in post office robberies.

Nielson was given a full life sentence, and died on the 18th December 2011.

May he rot in hell.

BICYCLES, GARDENS
AND ALLOTMENTS

In my 4 years working at Rolls Royce, I couldn't help but notice, even though we were making the best car in the world, most locals came to work on push bikes, and loved gardening, or they had an allotment. The bikes were just an observation, but the gardening bit got me thinking. About 12 years before, my dad found a place in Derbyshire that had mountains of spent mushroom compost that they just wanted to get rid of. I thought that all these gardeners in Crewe would love this gold standard compost.

When we had moved into our new house, it was the last house in the cul-de-sac, and next to it was a plot of land that wasn't big enough for the builders to fit a pair of semi-detached houses on.

I hired a big high sided coal wagon, just the same as my dad had done 12 years earlier, and went and fetched a load of this compost, and had it tipped on the land at the side of our house. I loved money, and they loved their garden, it was a match made in heaven.

Each day I would take 12 bags of compost in my car, £1-50 for 4 bags and deliver them. My boss was one of my best customers. One day I was asked to go to see the man in the personnel department, he was the one who had made it so hard for me to convince him I wanted the job. I sat opposite him at the table, he just said, I believe you are selling mushroom compost, I said, yes, but I am doing it in my spare time, he just said, I know, I would like 8 bags. So, I found myself delivering compost to the posh part of Crewe. I was making around £20 per week from this little venture, this was equal to half my wages that I was getting from Rolls Royce.

MY DAD AND ME WORKING TOGETHER AT ROLLS ROYCE.

1975 arrived with Kath and Harry moving into their new bungalow, and my mum and dad moving into the house they had built. We all now lived within walking distance of each other.

My dad had just been made redundant from Foden's, they manufactured Dumper Trucks, he had worked there for 20 years. It was a bit of an acrimonious parting, my dad could be a cantankerous man, and he was the works convenor, the union representative. Regardless of the years served, Foden's found a loop hole to make him redundant. Normally my dad would have fought this tooth and nail, but he was offered £1,000 in a redundancy payment. This would be a big help with the costs incurred in building their house, so he accepted it without much of a fight, [money talks]

He had been out of work for about 3 months, when I found out that Rolls Royce were setting on mechanical fitters, the same job my dad had done for most of his working life. So, I went to see my new friend, the personnel manager, and got my dad an interview. He was definitely well qualified for the job, and it was arranged for him to start work the following Monday. We travelled together on his first day, and I was able to show him around and take him to the department he would be working on. It felt so good that I was able to help him to get this job. At lunch time I took him to the canteen, he seemed quite happy how things had gone. When we got back from our lunch break my dad found all his tools and belongings had been taken to the security gate, and someone was standing by his workbench to escort him off the factory.

It all seemed very cloak and dagger, but we eventually found out that the union he was a member of, had gone to the Rolls Royce management, and told them that they thought my dad would be a trouble maker. Rolls Royce had rung Foden's to ask their opinion, their reply didn't go well for my dad. So, he only managed to work for Rolls Royce for 4 hours.

Understandably, I felt embarrassed and annoyed. The next day I went to see the personnel manager to vent my anger at how they had treated my dad. To be fair to him, he said he hadn't been consulted about the situation, and decisions like that would have come from much higher up. My dad took it better than me, but he never worked as a Fitter again.

Now he was back unemployed, he started to make garden fencing. The sectional garage he had built many years earlier, was now in the back garden of their new house, and he used this as his workshop to make the fencing. He was doing quite well, selling them through adverts in the local paper.

Even though I was now married, I still got called on by my dad to help with deliveries at weekends. This didn't go down well with Pat; I would get the dreaded look when I told her I would be helping with these deliveries. As normal, I never got paid for my labours, but occasionally the customers would ask if I would erect their fencing. This proved to be quite profitable for me.

MORE MONEY AND SAD NEWS

After 4 years working on the inspection department, where I had mostly enjoyed my time, and making lots of new

211

friends. My move to the small department assembling the Rolls Royce dashboards, had one major advantage, I had quite a big pay increase, because it was deemed a skilled job and carried a lot of responsibility, but with just 4 other men working in a very small room that had no windows was quite depressing. The other 4 men were much older than me, and they had worked together for years, so I felt a little bit like the outsider. The set up in this room, was, we all worked in a row, so all I could see was the back of the man in front of me. The concentration involved in the job didn't allow for any sort of conversation with the others, and I didn't have much in common with them anyway.

It was while I was working in this department that I got a message telling me to report to the main reception by the entrance to the factory. It was quite a long walk, and all sorts of things were going through my mind as to what I could have done wrong to be asked to go to this office.

As I walked in the room, one of the receptionists gave me a piece of paper with a phone number on it, she just said, your dad has been taken ill, and he is in hospital, you can use this phone to make your call. When I rang and gave my dad's name, I was told I should come to the hospital as soon as I could. The hospital was in Newcastle, the same hospital that Pat worked at, it was a 15-mile trip from Crewe. When I arrived, I managed to eventually find my mum, she told me my dad had had a heart attack, and was very poorly. After what seemed forever, a doctor came to us and said we could go to see him, he also said we should prepare ourselves for the worst. My dad wasn't aware that we were there, but we spent about half an hour with him. The doctor came to us again and said they would be performing a very risky operation, but if they didn't do it my dad would certainly die. They were going to do a triple heart bypass. In the 1970s this was quite a new procedure, and he had just a 10% chance of survival, and the next 48 hours would be the critical time.

It was a long night, but thankfully he made it through the operation, and spent the next two weeks in hospital. The day I went to pick him up from the hospital to take him home, he asked me to take him up a road that wasn't on our way home. When I asked him why, he just said he would tell me when we got there. The road was about two miles from the hospital and up a steep bank, at the top he asked me to pull over. He pointed to a building in the distance, I said, isn't that the hospital? He said from his hospital bed he could see this road that we were now parked on, and if he had the chance, he wanted to come up here and look back at the place he had spent the last two weeks.

My dad was never the same after the operation, as he would get all sorts of infections, and he never worked again. He was 53 years old when he had his heart attack. In time, he was able to drive, and do odd jobs around the house, but my poor mum, and at times me, were called upon to help even more than normal with whatever he decided to do.

ALL WORK AND NO PLAY

The 1960s had given me so much as a teenager, the music had been fantastic, the fashion was a big part of my 60s experience, and, of course seeing the Aliens transform into a thing of beauty. My social life was second to none, with so many friends sharing this wonderful decade, and in 1967 meeting Pat.

Now in the 1970s the music was changing, and even though there were some brilliant songs, it didn't seem to have the same excitement for me. The fashion was also changing, with platform shoes with bell bottom trousers. I rebelled against those for as long as I could, the girls were

213

wearing midi and maxi dresses, I mean, from a bloke's perspective this was terrible.

Now with a family, a mortgage, and all the bills that went with it, we were constantly broke. Pat was back working part time after having a few weeks off for maternity leave, and I was always trying to earn extra money in whatever way I could.

My dad couldn't make his fencing any longer after his heart attack, so, I started to miss out on the odd job that I would get when his customers wanted me to erect their fencing.

It got me thinking that maybe I could make garden fencing myself, and, I had seen, in a catalogue, some rustic garden furniture and trellising that looked simple to make. The only problem was that I would need money to buy the materials, and money was something I hadn't got. So, reluctantly I had to put the idea to one side, even though I thought I could make it pay.

One thing we had managed to buy was a second-hand fridge/freezer, it was about 6 feet tall. Our kitchen in the new house was much bigger than our last one, it had kitchen units on two walls and a dining table in the corner, so the only place for this fridge/freezer was on the back wall. It was very close to the door into the living room, in fact, you had to squeeze past it to get from the kitchen to the living room.

One Saturday morning Pat had gone to work, and I was sitting in the kitchen having a cup of tea. I was looking at this fridge/freezer wondering if there was somewhere else it could go. Then I had a eureka moment, behind the wall that it was standing by was our garage. I thought that if I cut a hole in the wall, then the bulk of this fridge/freezer could be pushed into the garage, leaving just the door flush with the wall in the kitchen. I went and got my bolster chisel and hammer, I drew a pencil line around the fridge/freezer, then dragged it out of the way and started to cut a hole in the back wall. As you can imagine, I was making a lot of mess and dust, so I went outside and opened the garage doors. I could then chuck the rubble into the garage and it would also help clear the dust. After about 2 hours I had got the hole cut out. I stood in the kitchen admiring my handy work, when Pat pulled into the drive, she sat in the car for quite a while just looking into the garage and the hole cut out in the back wall. When she eventually got out, I got the look that normally didn't require any words, but eventually she asked why could she see the kitchen sink through the back wall of the garage. After I put the fridge/freezer into the hole, just leaving the door flush with the kitchen wall, even Pat thought it looked ok. Its only when I tried to put the car in the garage, that I realised I couldn't quite shut the garage doors. From that day on I had to hold them closed with string - but we had a lot more room in the kitchen!

TIME FOR ANOTHER CHANGE

Stan and Hillary [the ones who painted their hall, stairs, and landing pillar box red] were down our house one night, and I started to tell Stan about my idea of making garden fencing and rustic garden furniture. Stan had now left his job as a figure painter, and for the last two years had been working for the gas board. Every home in the country was having its gas supply changed from normal gas, to North Sea Gas, but this contract was coming to an end. He seemed interested in my idea, and said he wouldn't mind having a go at it with me.

No matter how many plans we made, the lack of money was always the stumbling block. So, to get this idea up and running, we decided to go to the bank and ask for a business loan. We put all our plans down on a piece of paper to put to the bank manager, and we had worked out we would need about £1,000 to get us started. A few days later we both took a couple of hours off work, and went down to the bank. It's hard to believe this today, but we were able to walk into the bank without an appointment, and ask to see the manager. After 20 minutes or so, a young man invited us into a side room, and we put our proposal to him. Even though I was only 25 at that time, this young man seemed younger than me, he didn't look old enough to be a bank manager. He went over our ideas and finally said, if we opened a business account, he would transfer the loan. We came out of that meeting not quite believing it could be that easy.

The following day we got a call from the bank, asking us to call in as soon as possible. Both Stan and me made our excuses and finished work early the following day, and went back to the bank. This time the man we saw was much older, and looked more like a bank manager. He started off by apologising, and saying he had been off the day we came into the bank, and unfortunately there was a problem with our loan. His young deputy had forgotten to ask for surety against the loan. We asked what sort of surety he would need, well, he said, if you own your houses, we could use that. He pointed out this was normal practice, and that the building society would have priority over any debt, so we took out a £500 loan each, and now the £1,000 was paid into our business account.

Over the next few years this bank manager would come to my rescue in one of my darkest days.

Both Stan and me thought that until we got established, it was best if we did this business part time. We first looked for a workshop. We found a building about 2 miles from home, it was very cheap, but the reason it was cheap was because it was on the first floor, so everything had to be carried up a flight of steps. The next thing was to find businesses that supplied the materials we needed for the fencing and the rustic garden furniture. The materials for the fencing were easy, there were quite a few local firms we could get these from. The rustic poles, for the garden furniture on the other hand proved to be a problem. There was no Google back then, and there was no local supplier, so we went to the library and looked through phone books. Eventually we found a forestry commission near to the Scottish border that sold rustic poles. We rang them, and were told that because of the transport distance, we would have to order a full wagon load, and send a cheque for the full amount, which was almost half of our business loan. We went and bought a circular saw, and we found a very battered old pick-up truck that we got for £150. Now all we had to do was wait for the rustic poles to be delivered. The day it arrived was one of the hottest days of the year, both Stan and me had been waiting since 2 o'clock. The waggon eventually pulled into the yard at 6pm, it's hard to describe the look on our faces when we saw what was on the back of this waggon. It was like the biggest delivery of telegraph poles you had ever seen, totally the wrong sort of poles to make trellising and garden furniture. The delivery driver refused to take it back, and as we had already paid for it, we had no option but to accept it. It took us 2 hours to unload it. We got our totally inappropriate saw and started to cut these totally inappropriate poles into manageable lengths. By 10pm we were knackered, and went home utterly deflated. We went back the next day [Saturday] and we managed to cut off the top half of the poles [the thin bit] that we could use, and the rest we cut into 6 feet lengths. We thought we could sell those to farmers for fence posts.

The first thing we made were some garden benches, and through an advert we had put in the local paper, we got our first sale. We proudly delivered it, and went home with the £8 we had charged. About an hour after we got back, we got a phone call from the customer. He said his wife had sat on the bench, "and to quote his words", she has got splinters in her backside. He wanted us to take it back and refund his money. Not the best start to our business, but I have to say I had that bench at home for many years with no problem.

We also were able to make quite a lot of rustic trellising and arches, and we did do very well out of these. Trying to sell the 6 feet posts to the farmers wasn't easy, as you can imagine, the farmers weren't going to part with their money without a lot of negotiation. I'm pretty sure we didn't make a profit from the farmers, but we were happy just to break even.

After a month or so we had managed to sell most of the trellising and arches, and made a small profit. To be honest we were relieved just to get our money back.

We didn't go down that route again, we decided that we should concentrate on making the standard garden fencing, and if the customer wanted it erecting, we would also do that.

After 5 years working for Rolls Royce, I had enjoyed the first 4 years, but now assembling the dashboards to these very posh cars in a small workshop with no windows, wasn't exactly something I looked forward to long term.

I was starting to enjoy working outside again. I said to Stan one Sunday night, that I would be handing in my notice on Monday morning, and start to do this fencing full time. Stan didn't seem too keen, and who could blame him, it wasn't exactly the flying start we had hoped for. I did say to him that I would prefer it to be the two of us, but if he didn't fancy it, then I would do it on my own.

The next day I gave my notice letter to my boss, he wasn't impressed, and thought I was mad to give up a secure job for this. He did say he would hang on to my letter until lunch time, to give me chance to think about it, but I went through with it, and went home not sure if I would be doing it on my own, or, if I would have a partner. Thankfully, Stan came down to tell me he had also handed in his notice, so in one weeks' time we would start to work for ourselves.

Joanne, our daughter, and her friend Paul, sitting on the first rustic bench we had made. This was the bench our very first customer asked us to take back, because, he said his wife had got splinters in her backside after sitting on it.

Joanne survived without getting any splinters, and we had this bench for many years without the need for tweezers! The following Monday we went to Fields Road in Alsager, they had units to rent that were more suitable for what we needed. So, we started our first week as self-employed fencing manufacturers, and it felt good.

We spent the first two days setting up our workshop, and we also had a dipping tank made, that was 7ft square and 1ft deep, this was to dip the panels in creosote after we had made them. We were more careful of what we ordered this time, we had one local timber yard who cut all our framework to exact sizes, and another timber yard in Stoke who supplied the waney edged boards, so this time there were no surprises when they were delivered. As expected, our first week was slow as far as sales were concerned. We spent quite a bit of time going to sectional building firms and garden centres, and it wasn't long before we had lots of orders coming in from these outlets, their orders could be anything from 30 fencing panels to over 100.

We also advertised in the local paper, so we were getting orders from the public too, and many of them would ask us to erect the fencing for them. Just to keep up with the orders our working day would start at 7am and finish around 8pm. Up to now we had been hand nailing every panel, but one day not long after we had started, a rep from a firm came to see us. He wanted to demonstrate a nailing gun, that he said would speed up our production, to be honest we were a bit sceptical about his claims, but he offered to provide us with a nailing gun, a small compressor, and a box of the special nails for a few days for us to try out. On average a 6ft x 4ft panel would take us about 20 minutes to make, now with this nailing gun we could do the same job in about 5 minutes, so it was a no brainer. We ordered two guns and a few boxes of nails, and then went to buy a much bigger compressor.

At the end of each day, the last job was to dip all the panels that we had made into the creosote bath, and leave them on the draining board overnight. I remember after one very long day, both Stan and me thought we deserved a pint. We called into our local pub and stood by the bar with our drink, it soon became obvious we were standing at the bar on our own. Everyone had moved as far away from us as possible, the smell of the creosote on our clothes was overpowering to everyone except us.

Pat would make me stand outside the back door and strip off, before I was allowed into the house, and she also complained that after she had washed these smelly clothes, she would have to put the washer on again with no clothes in it just to get rid of the smell. After spending over 12 hours at work and then coming home smelling of creosote,

I wasn't very popular with Pat. It took us about 6 months to find an alternative to creosote, it was a water-based wood preservative that didn't smell ☐. So, I gained a few Brownie points with Pat for that.

We did find time to have some fun, this photo was taken in Pete and Sylv's house. On the left is Pete, as Boy George, then me as Al Capone, third from the left is Stan, my business partner, he came as a Vicar and for some reason he decided to bring his Saxophone, then on the right is Pat, as Hilder Ogden [Coronation Street].

When I got through the madness of the first few months of working for myself, that took up far too much of my time. We would spend many weekends with Pete and Sylv, either going for weekend's away, or on Holiday together, or going down to the park playing tennis

You never know what could happen when you are digging a hole for a fence post.

I wasn't exactly, what you would call the family man at this time of my life. It was work, work, and more work. I would get home and Joanne would be in bed, and I would leave for work the next morning before she had got up, and I wasn't giving Pat much, if any of my time. The difference from having a 9 to 5 job and working for yourself was massive, each day you woke up, unless you went out and earned your living, then no one was going to pay you. So, this was a very hard time for Pat.

Why hadn't this idiot stayed in a secure job? There were days when I thought the same, but would never admit it, but I couldn't have asked for a better business partner than Stan. We never fell out or had any major disagreements, ok, sometimes I would have to bite my lip, and I'm sure he did the same, but we got on well.

One of our neighbours had asked us to instal some fencing in their back garden. It was on this day that Pat had to waddle across the road to the neighbour's house that we were working on. I was digging a post hole when I looked up to see Pat standing there. She just said, It's Time To Go, NOW!!

So, I put my spade down and helped Pat back across the road, and we got into the car and made our way to the Maternity hospital. I know, who would have thought it, but somehow, I must have found the time.

223

On the way to the Hospital, I started to wonder if we would be in for another marathon session, like with Joannes birth.

We got to the Hospital around 4pm, and this time we were put into delivery room number 8. When Pat had our first bundle of joy, the midwife taking care of her was Gwyneth, who Pat had trained with, and we had become good friends with her and her husband. This time the midwife in charge of Pats care, was an imposing figure, who the students and midwives knew not to cross. She had originated from Jamaica, her name was Clarissa, and was a Senior Sister on the delivery ward. If she told me to jump, I was fully prepared to ask how high.

Everything was moving along fine; I would go to the reception every now and then to phone everyone with a progress report.

Clarissa was very quickly gaining my admiration, she was so calm and reassuring, explaining to me how things were going. The delivery was moving along quite fast, it was almost midnight on the 27th October, and Clarissa told Pat that the head was visible and to start pushing. Pat looked at the clock on the wall, and it was 11-50, she then said to Clarissa, can I just hang on another few minutes, both me and the midwife looked at each other, she said to Pat, why? Pat explained, that it had been her dad's birthday on the 26th and he had so wanted his grandchild to be born on his birthday if possible. So, having missed his birthday, Pat also preferred an even number, and if she could hang on a few minutes, it would be the 28th. So, Clarissa said, OK, I will give you the time it takes me to clean my trolley, then madam, you will have this baby.

Tracey Michelle was born at 3 minutes past 12 on the 28th October 1976 weighing 7lbs 2oz and she was perfect.

So, there you have it, our family was now complete.

Joanne saying hello, for the first time, to her little sister, Tracey.

Aunty Ann, having her first cuddle.

Back at work we decided that along with fencing, we should try our hand at making garden sheds. When we delivered the fencing orders to the Garden Centres, we would go and look at the sheds they had on display, just to give us an idea how they were made. We soon realised that no matter what size shed we looked at, the basic principle of construction was the same. We went and bought a 4ft x 4ft shed, so we could copy the method. Within 6 months of us buying this shed we were making an average of 10 sheds a day, and were now employing 6 people, 4 of them were joiners, one was a labourer and one to do the deliveries. Most of the sheds and fencing, around 75% were being bought in bulk by the Garden Centres, and the rest were to the public.

We stayed on the industrial estate in Alsager, but moved into a much bigger workshop. The orders for the sheds were coming in faster than we could make them. We put an advert in the local paper for another joiner, and we had quite a few applicants. One man came across well, he was in his late 40s and seemed enthusiastic, I took him around the workshop, explaining how we did the different jobs, then we sat down in our little office, and I told him we paid the joiners on peace work, so he would be paid ex amount on the sheds he completed. He was happy with that, but I did notice that he kept his right hand in his jacket pocket throughout the interview.

On the Monday morning our new recruit turned up on time, and I took him to the workshop and went over how things were done. No one needed any tools, we provided everything, by now we had rip saws, cross cut saws and the magical nailing guns that were the way these sheds could be produced much faster. I showed him to his workbench, and gave him a cutting list for what I thought was the easiest shed to make. I then picked up some framework and gave it to him, but he fumbled and dropped it. It was only then that I realised we had employed a one-handed joiner. He had lost his hand in an accident with a circular saw, so not a good start. He tried to convince me he could do the job, but I had my doubts. I gave him a week to prove me wrong, but that was 6 days to long. I felt sorry for him, but there was no way he could do the job. So, from now on, I would have to see both hands before I gave anyone a job.

PARTY TIME, AND MEETING THE NEIGHBOURS

Apart from Stan and Hilary, and our next-door neighbour, we didn't really know anyone else in our little cul-de-sac, we would say hello to them if we saw them either cleaning their car or mowing the front lawn. Most of our neighbours were of a similar age to us, apart from the couple who lived directly opposite, I would say they were in their 50s.

Joe, our next-door neighbour had moved to England from Greece. I do remember asking him if Joe was his birth name, as it didn't sound very Greek, he just laughed and said, no one could pronounce his Greek name, including his wife, so she called him Joe, and it had stuck.

Joe told me he had sent his dad, "who still lived in a place called Halkidiki, in main land Greece," a photo of his house and in the photo, you could see the small wooded area at the end of our cul-de-sac. When his dad replied to the letter, he asked Joe, as you live next to a forest, do you have any problem with the Monkeys damaging the house. Apparently, his dad must have thought England, had gangs of Monkeys roaming round.

It was now June 1977, one of our neighbours suggested we should organise a street party, to celebrate our Queens silver jubilee. A little committee got together to organise it, and on the day of the party we all dragged our kitchen tables and chairs outside and they were filled with food and drink. It started with all the young children having a sack race and other games, then someone suggested that the adults should take part in a few games too. I can highly recommend parties like this if you want to get to know your neighbours, especially if someone's wife who I had probably only said hello to a couple of times, now has her right leg strapped to my left leg, in the 3-legged race, or when a stranger gets hold of your ankles in the wheelbarrow race. Then someone got all the men to stand in a line, and we were told to roll our trouser legs up above our knees, and the women walked up and down the line looking very carefully at our legs, then they all stood in a huddle whispering and giggling. Eventually one of them announced that out of the 10 men in the line, I had won the knobbly knees competition. I'm not sure how that happened, as Pat had always told me I had nice legs, but I was awarded a jubilee tankard, so I graciously excepted my prize. As it started to get dark, one of the neighbours went and got a big mettle drum from their garden and we lit a fire in it. We were soon running out of firewood, so Stan and me went to our workshop in the pickup truck, and brought back a mountain of wood offcuts. So now it was more like a bonfire, and the party went on late into the night. The following morning, we all started to get our road back to normal, its only then that we noticed our fire had melted a big hole in the tarmac. Eventually the council came out and repaired the damage, no one admitted to it, but we all had a good day and night.

This one little party, turned a road of strangers into good friends.

Top photo, left, many cakes were made to celebrate this special occasion. Top right, our city was the largest manufacturer of commemorative plates and tankards like the one I won for the knobbly knee's competition. Bottom photo, the children ready to start their sack race.

WE ARE OFF TO IRAN FOR 18 MONTHS!

This was what Harry [Pat's dad] announced to us in 1977.
Not long after Tracey was born, Harry got the opportunity
to go to work in Iran. The Iranians had built a new sanitary
manufacturing factory, and Harry's job would be to teach
the locals the skills of his trade, and I can't think of anyone
better than Harry to do a job like this. The big down side to
it was that the contract was for 18 months, and Kath would
be going with him.
Iran in 1977 was a totally different country than it is today.
Harry had worked for Twyford's, in Alsager as a sanitary
caster, this was probably one of the most physical jobs you
could imagine. Harry's physique gave the appearance that
he had spent hours in the gym, but this couldn't be further
from the truth. All his hard, physical work had its
advantages, his pay-packet at the end of the week gave him
probably double the average wage at that time.
One thing he wasn't good at was managing his money, but
Kath was totally the opposite, so, like the good husband,
Harry would give Kath his wage packet each week, and she
would give him a few pounds back, he jokingly called it his
pocket money. Each Saturday he would walk down to his
dads, and together they would sit and study the form, they
both loved a little flutter on the horses, and as his dad
couldn't get out anymore due to his stroke, Harry would
take their bets to the Bookies, they didn't go mad, it would
be just a few shillings, then he would go in the pub for a
pint. With Kath holding the purse strings, so to speak, this
was how Harry could afford to buy a new car every couple
of years, and how they could afford to buy their caravan.
Going to Iran wasn't something they chose lightly, they had
a plan, and that was, after their 18 months in Iran, they had

worked out that they would be able to pay off their mortgage.

Included in the contract, the Iranians provided them with a brand-new Bungalow. It was in its own compound, and along with 2 other Brits, who would work alongside Harry. It had its own swimming pool, and they each had a car and a driver to take them to the factory each morning, and on any shopping or sightseeing trips. This was a wonderful opportunity, but very sad for us, as they were a big part of our lives, and we would all miss them very much. They did come back on occasions for holidays, and Harry would only speak kindly about the Iranian workers. He said they treated both Kath and himself like they were celebrities, and they were very often invited to their homes for a meal, and would be invited to local sporting events as guest of honour.

Towards the end of the contract, it all started to go wrong. It was around February 1979 that Harry was told by the workers, that they thought he should get out of the country as fast as possible. Firstly, he sent Kath home, but there were things he needed to sort out before he left. He was still owed quite a bit of money, and spent a few days sorting it out, but it soon became obvious that he had to leave. The Shah had been deposed and had left the country, and now the Ayatollah Khomeini had taken over. One of the workers, who had become friends with Harry, put him in the back of his car, and told him to keep his head down, and he drove him to the airport. I think it's safe to say Harry got out just in time, but they did manage to pay off their mortgage.

Harry inside the sanitary manufacturing factory with one of
his new Iranian friends

Top - Harry as guest of honour with the team, and
Bottom - presenting the trophy to the winners.
It's a shame it couldn't be like that today.

234

If Harry's final few days in Iran had been a little traumatic, it wasn't going to put him off. In 1981 he got a similar job, but this time in Saudi Arabia. He decided that it was best if he went on his own as the contract was for a shorter time. Also, his accommodation would be just a hotel room, so, Kath stayed at home. In his letters sent back to us, it was obvious that he wasn't enjoying this trip, but he stuck it out and finished the contract.

His final trip working abroad was a much better experience. He headed off to Trinidad and Tobago, the factory he was to help set up was on the smaller island of Tobago. He would send letters home, telling us that he felt like he was working in paradise. This time he shared a bungalow with 2 other Brits, and said it overlooked a beautiful bay, and he would sit in the garden having his breakfast, looking at the Humming Birds just a few feet away.

Before I finish with Harrys travels, I remember in 1968, I had only been going out with Pat for 12 months. I was sitting in their kitchen, when both Kath and Harry came and sat with me, I thought, oops, what have I done now. They started off by telling me that they were thinking of emigrating to Australia. Some of you may remember, there was an offer that they called, the £10 Poms. This was basically, the Australian government trying to attract Brits to move there. Kath said, they both understood how close Pat and me were, and suggested that I should go with them. Pat also said she didn't want to go without me. After about a week of this floating around in my head, I agreed. It was all getting sorted, when they found out that I could end up being conscripted into the Australian Army, as they were involved in the Vietnam war. Thankfully, they said they couldn't risk it, so, if I couldn't go, then they wouldn't go either, Phew.

1979 WAS A FUNNY YEAR

BUT I DIDN'T DO A LOT OF LAUGHING

At work we were very busy, but we weren't making our fortune. The problem with supplying most of our sheds and fencing to Garden Centres was that they wanted everything at rock bottom prices. I don't think things have change too much even today. The manufacturer ends up selling a lot, but with little return, but you get into a situation where you must keep going to pay the bills.

Someone once said to me, "anyone can be a busy fool". Pat was at home looking after Joanne and Tracey, so we only had what I was earning. It was hard times, but I never regretted what I was doing.

Even before my mum and dad had built their house, it had always been my ambition that one day we would build our own. We had been married for less than 12 months, when we went to look at a plot of land that was just down the road from us. The views from this plot were fantastic, so, we went to see the farmer who's land it belonged to. It wasn't up for sale as a building plot, we just loved the area. The farmer said that he was happy for us to buy the plot. Thankfully back then applying for planning permission was free, so we put in our application. It took 8 weeks for the council to turn it down, stating that it was on green belt. In hindsight it was probably for the best, as I doubt, we could have afforded the building costs let alone have the money to buy the land. It was just a dream, but it was always in the back of my mind that one day we could do it. This was in 1971, fast forward to 1979. One Saturday, Kath and Harry went to visit Ann and John, and on the way, they passed a sign advertising 3 building plots for sale. The following day they told us about these plots, and Harry said that he was thinking of going for one, so, we all went to have a look. The plots were a good size, and most importantly they were flat, and had good open views from the back. I suggested to Pat that we should go for one of these plots too. First, I got the look that normally was enough to let me know what she thought, but this time, it was followed up with No, No and No. She loved the house we were now living in, and, also, even though she loved her mum and dad, she didn't want to live next door to them. I did my best to change her mind, but I wasn't getting anywhere. Then Kath and Harry found out that the plot they wanted had a large water culvert [a big water pipe] running to one side of the plot, so they pulled out of the sale. I thought they would go for one of the other plots, but Harry said they had decided to stay where they were.

Now, when Harry told me this, I thought it was worth trying to convince Pat that we should go for the middle plot. I think it was more me grinding her down, rather than what she really wanted to do, and that was to stay in the house she loved, but she eventually said yes. So, we put our house up for sale, and within 3 hours of the sales board being put up, a man came knocking on the door. He had a look round, and just said he wanted it. He told us he had just moved back from living in Sri Lanka, where he said he had owned two cinemas, but he had sold them, and wanted to move back to the UK to retire. He also said it would be a cash sale, and agreed the asking price of £15,500. When he told us it would be a cash sale, we never imagined he would turn up the next day with £15,500 in cash in a suitcase.

I don't know how business transactions were done in Sri Lanka, but here we had to go through the normal procedures. So, now, much sooner than we could have imagined, our house was sold.

After we had paid our mortgage off, we were left with £10,000. The plot of land was £6,500, so the simple maths tells you we had £3,500 left, obviously, we would need a mortgage to help with the building of the house.

Sometimes I should question my own sanity, and this was one of those times. We now had a plot of land and no house, with two children who hadn't even started school yet. The only option was to get a caravan to live in until the house was finished. At this time, I don't think I had many Brownie points as far as Pat was concerned, but the mention of living in a caravan, put me on minus points.

We eventually found a caravan; it was about 20 miles away, it was a massive, 46ft long [14 meters] Pats first comment was," it's a dump". I couldn't argue with that, but I just said, yes, but it's a long dump. It was so long that it was designed to be towed in two separate sections. We paid £600 for it, including delivery, and we put it at the back of our plot. I put the two halves together, but the land was on a bit of a slope, so, to go from the living room to the bedroom was a bit uphill, and each morning it was a quick jog down to the living room, but now we had a roof over our heads. The first thing I did was have a trench dug from the road, and we managed to get an electrical supply to the caravan, but the waterboard were not quite so helpful. They wouldn't give us a direct supply; all they could offer was a water bowser that was left at the top of the building site. So, to start with, we had to carry tubs of water from the bowser to the caravan.

Our 46ft long caravan, or as Pat liked to call it, our Dump in a field. It had a good-sized living room, a separate kitchen, a bathroom and two bedrooms.

A bit of child labour, Joanne fetching water from the bowser. She just wanted to help, Honest!

I put fencing around the caravan, to keep the girls safe and included swings a slide. The shed I made, in the photo below, inspired me to change things for the better at work.

The same time that we moved into the caravan, at work we were having problems with cash flow. We were selling lots of sheds and fencing, but the garden centres, who were our main outlet, would want any orders they placed with us delivered as soon as possible, but then could take 2 months to settle their bill. Both Stan and me were spending valuable work time chasing outstanding invoices.

Our bank manager was constantly on our back, telling us we must get our overdraft down, our accountant was saying the same. It finally came to a head, when the bank manager rang us to say, he had spoken to our accountant, and had arranged a meeting at the bank, and we should all meet there the following day at 2 o'clock. Both Stan and me arrived on time, and were asked to take a seat outside the bank managers door. We sat there for about 20 minutes, then the door opened and we were invited in. I was shocked, and annoyed to see our accountant was already in the room. They had both been discussing our business, and deciding what to do, while Stan and me had been sat outside. They had concluded that the only way was for us to declare bankruptcy. For me, with just a plot of land, and my family in a caravan, this was not an option. The conversation got heated to say the least, the bank previously held the deeds to our house, now they had the deeds to our plot of land.

In just two days' time Pat and me had an appointment with the building society, to apply for a mortgage, so we could get on with building our house. One thing they had asked for was to see the deeds to our plot of land.

I argued with the bank manager and our accountant that we could turn it around, they were not convinced, but we refused to do it their way. I knew I was on a sticky wicket with my next request. I said, that I needed the bank to release the deeds to the land, so that I could take them to the building society, just for the day, then I would return them the following day. He said that this was not possible, given that we were £10,000 over drawn. I said that without them, it would be impossible for us to get the mortgage we needed. He said, the only way he could do it, was for me to give him an alternative surety until I returned the land deeds.

The meeting ended, and I went home with my head spinning, was I about to lose the land and caravan, our only assets. That night I stood outside the caravan, looking through the window at Pat and the girls, I just didn't know what to do.

I will never know how I got there, but I ended up outside Kath and Harrys bungalow. [Pats parents] I honestly don't remember walking down there; it was a good 2 miles from the caravan. I went in and started to explain my problem, this was something I hadn't even told Pat yet. Without a single second's thought, Harry said he trusted that I would turn it around, and he said, we could use the deeds to their bungalow as surety, until we got the mortgage.

I went to the bank the following day, and put this idea to the bank manager, he just said, you must have very supportive in-laws. He then did something I had not expected, he said he would release our land deeds for 24 hours, if I promised to bring them back the next day, without the need to use Kath and Harrys deeds. This was a very good gesture on his part, and a massive relief to me

The following day we went to the building society to ask for our mortgage. We explained that we had £3,500 left from the sale of our house, and that would be enough to buy the bricks and put the concrete slab in.

One of the first questions he asked us, was, "Have you ever been declared bankrupt"? I thought Pat was going to fall off her chair, but I quickly said no, well up to now, I hadn't.

Funnily enough the amount of mortgage we were asking for, was £10,000, the same amount that our business was in debt for. The other questions after the bankruptcy one were quite straight forward, and we came out of that meeting with our mortgage. The first thing I did was to go to the bank, and hand back the land deeds. I don't know who was the most relieved, me, for managing to get a mortgage, or my bank manager, for getting our land deeds back.

He was putting his neck on the block, helping me out like this. I did say to him, that I was determined to get our business back on track, we shook hands, and he just said, I hope so.

The one big difference to getting a mortgage when you are building a house, is, they only give you bits of the money after you have completed each section. We had put in the concrete base, and bought all the bricks with our own money. They would then release a small amount of money so we could do the next section, then they would send someone out to inspect it. It was mostly just a formality, but it was always a nervous time, until they agreed everything had been done to their satisfaction

My brother-in-law John, was a digger driver, and did a great job in digging our footings out. I was doing as many jobs as I could on our new house, just to save money. So, when the reinforcing bars were delivered, I started to wire them together, but before I could get the reinforcing into the footings it started to rain, and it rained for 3 days none stop. The footings were now full to the top with water, I managed to borrow a pump, but no matter how fast I pumped it out it would just fill up again. I gave up and sat in the caravan looking at this 3ft deep water in the footings that took the shape of our house. Then I had an idea, if I knocked 4ft long pegs into the footings, about 10ft apart, and put a pencil mark at the top of the water line, it would give me a perfect level, [the water acted like a massive spirit level]. So, you can see after all the shit in my life at this time, there were some good moments, well I had to hang on to the simple pleasures.

THE RAIN HELPED TO ANSWER OUR PROBLEMS AT WORK.

It was Sunday, and another one of those rainy days where I couldn't do much on our building site, so I decided to go to our workshop and make a shed, so that I could store things like bags of cement. I also made a canopy to fit over the caravan entrance, so that we could put a few things outside, like muddy boots and other messy things that Pat was constantly moaning about. She would say, it's hard enough trying to keep this place tidy, without you coming in and walking mud everywhere! After I put up the canopy, I then erected the shed in the rain. When I finished, I sat inside the shed admiring my handywork. I was frustrated that it was too wet on the site to do anything, so I started to work out how much it had cost to make the shed. The next day, Monday, I compared the cost of the shed I had made in comparison to what we were selling them to the garden centres. It soon became clear that, even though we had costed the sheds out as far as materials were concerned, there were other overheads that we had naively not considered. That same day, unusually, both Stan and me had taken a large shed out together. After the shed was delivered and erected, we did something else that normally we wouldn't dream of doing, and that was to go to a pub, for a pie and a pint. It was over this lunch break that we made the decision to stop supplying all the garden centres, and concentrate on just supplying our sheds and fencing to the public. Up to now, if someone from the public wanted a shed, we would have to say there was a 4 to 6 week waiting time, so more often than not they would go elsewhere for their shed. So, we were turning away the orders that made the most profit. The garden centres were constantly trying to get a better price from us, so telling them that we wouldn't be supplying them anymore was the easy bit, the hard part was having to lay off some of our workforce. By now, we had 4 joiners, one lad making fencing, and another who would do most of the deliveries. It wasn't the easiest thing to do, but we had no choice, we finished all 4 joiners, as, to be honest you didn't need to be a joiner to make a shed. Now we could concentrate on just public sales, and instead of telling them it would be 4 to 6 weeks, we could now tell them it was 4 to 6 days. At last, we weren't busy fools anymore, we were starting to make a good profit.

The two lads we had now working with us, were well worth our trust in keeping them on. Nigel and Carl had helped us to keep going, and by the time we reached 12 months from the dark time when we were advised to go bankrupt by our bank manager and accountant, we reached our target, and even better. We had managed to pay back the £10,000 that we were in dept for, and, not only that, but had made a very healthy profit. To their credit, both our bank manager and our accountant congratulated us.

Years later I was invited to a promotional evening at the bank, the idea was to get local businesses meeting each other. I got talking to the bank manager, and he said he still tells new businesses our story of survival, but I doubt he tells them the story of him releasing our land deeds for that very important 24 hours, so we could get our mortgage. I will be forever grateful to him for that.

AT THIS SAME TIME, I HADN'T ONLY GOT A BUSINESS TO RESCUE, BUT A HOUSE TO BUILD.

Our house was coming along, and we reached the point where we could have all the utilities connected to the house. At the start of our building work, the only thing we had managed to do was to have a trench dug from the road to lay the electric cable in, this allowed us to have electric in our caravan. Now the water board and gas board said that we would need to open the trench that the electric cable was in, and all three services could go in the same trench. This was brilliant news, I thought at last, we could have a water supply to the caravan, and not have to carry tubs of water from the bowser. I ran a temporary water pipe to the caravan, Pat was getting excited at the thought of, at last, after 7 months, she would have running-water in the van.

The big turn on day arrived, and Pat stood in the caravan kitchen, by the sink tap ready to turn it on. I said I would go to the road and turn on the water. I shouted down to Pat, ok, I'm Turning It On, I could hear Pat shouting back, but I couldn't work out what she was saying, so, I walked back to the van, only to see her standing in the doorway, looking like she had just had a shower fully clothed. We hadn't realised that above the sink there was a galvanised water tank and it was full of holes. It was like someone had shot it with a machine gun. I got one of those looks from Pat that didn't need any words, but two days later, all was fixed, and we had running water in the van.

We obviously tried to do as much as we could ourselves to save money. I had managed to get all the windows at a bargain price, they were Georgian style. I suggested to Pat that we could glaze them. So, with all the glass cut, we started. I was putting the putty in the rebates and Pat had a little hammer and panel pins to hold the glass in place. I think we spent 3 nights doing this and only managed to do 5 windows. It was so cold, our hands were freezing, and Pat was hitting her fingers with the hammer more than hitting the panel pins. So, yet another one of Pats looks along with the odd swear words convinced me to get a glazier in to finish it off, he completed the rest of the windows in just a few hours. Another lesson learned.

We were getting very close to finishing the house and started to collect our furniture from friends and relatives who had kindly stored them for us. All I had left to do was to fit some of the internal doors and put floorboards down in the bathroom, when Pat came and told me the calor-gas had run out in the caravan. So, we decided to just move in that night. it was the 8th May 1980, and just 11 months since we had first moved into the caravan.

I put a few loose boards over the joists in the bathroom turned on the bath tap, and for the first time in 11 months we had hot running water. I lit a fire in our sitting room, and the 4 of us sat cross legged on the floor, and did toast on the open fire. It was the best feeling and the best toast ever.

This was at about the time I thought it would be a good idea to try and put the glass in our Georgian windows ourselves to save money. It was freezing cold, so not my best idea.

Me and a friend putting the roof trusses on.

You can also see part of our caravan, on the right of the photo [or as Pat called it, our Dump in a field,] along with the shed, and the canopy I put over the entrance to the caravan, that was our home for 11 months.

When we moved in, and because it was a self-build, we could claim back all the VAT that we had paid on materials to build the house. So, one of the first things we did was to go through every invoice, this was a mammoth task, but well worth it, we calculated we could claim back £1,000, we felt rich.

Just a few days after we had moved in, we got a knock on our door. It was the lady who we had bought the building plot from, she asked us if we would be interested in buying all the field at the back of our house. It was 11 acres, and she wanted £11,000 for it. Obviously, we couldn't afford it, and even if we could, I didn't know what we could do with 11 acres of farm land. The next day I was thinking about this land, and I had an idea, so, I went to see her and asked if she would be prepared to sell us just one acre that was directly behind our house, for £1,000. She agreed, so our £1,000 VAT money was spent almost as soon as we had got it, what we were going to do with it was for another day.

IT WAS A BIT OF A SURPRISE, BUT I UNDERSTOOD

My business partner, Stan, came to me one day and said that he wanted to go on his own, just making fencing. I must admit I was a bit surprised, we had gone through some difficult times together, especially through the threat of bankruptcy, but we came out the other side much stronger. Stan and me over the 4 years we had worked together had never fallen out, in fact considering what we had been through I think we had got closer as friends. I was always more interested in the sectional building side of our business and Stan was more involved with the fencing side. So, in a way I could understand his thinking, and I wasn't going to stand in his way. We made an agreement, that, if I wanted any fencing I would buy it from him, and vice versa if he sold a shed, he would get it from me. He decided to just work by himself, and the two lads, Nigel and Carl would stay with me.

Stan took on a small unit on the site that we had worked on throughout our 4 years together, and I found a workshop about 5 miles away, in a place called Biddulph. After the initial shock of being the only one to make the decisions, I found it quite liberating, and, also, I had two lads working with me who were just as determined to make it work.

It's at this time, 1981, that the country went into a recession, and listening to the News I started to get quite concerned, but it worked in my favour, people stopped moving house, and started spending their money on home improvements, so our shed sales increased. Stan and me had stuck to our agreement, but after about 12 months Stan packed in his fencing business, so I was back making sheds and fencing. We got so busy that I had to employ more people, but this time I was making money, so it made sense to take advantage of a growing market. John was the first one I employed, he was the husband of one of Pats cousins, then the next to join the workforce Glenn, he was Pats cousin. Then we had the miners' strike, and Pats brother was one of those on strike, so, he came to work for me for the duration of the dispute, which seemed to go on for months. So, you can see, there was a bit of a theme going on. It could have been a bit risky, employing 3 family members, but it worked out well, and everyone got on. Now, including me there were 6 of us, and the old battered pick-up truck that I had used from the start, was becoming more of a problem rather than an asset, so it was sent to the scrap yard. I replaced it with a pick-up truck that the council were selling, it was only 6 months old, but one truck wasn't coping with the deliveries, so I invested in a

251

second truck, this one was brand new, and I was able to buy both outright, with no finance. Also, at the same time we bought our first new car, it was a Nisan Bluebird.

The yellow pick-up that I bought from the council; I got it for a fraction of the cost of a new one. The blue one, I had made with a wider back to carry bigger sheds. I had it made with a tipper back, this was more to do with jobs I was doing at home rather than work. Brian on the left, then Carl, and John, 3 of the lads who worked for me at the time.

Two of the sectional buildings we were making at that
time.
Top photo, a Pidgeon Loft. Bottom photo, this was to be a
snooker room in someone's back garden.

Above, Our first new car, a Nisan Bluebird.

Now we had moved into our house, we put the caravan up for sale. A young couple who were about to build their own house came to look at it. When I said that it had been brilliant for us, I'm glad they didn't see the look I got from Pat.

Amazingly, we got £600, the same price that we had paid for it. We got a local farmer with his tractor to tow it to the road, and watched as it was put on a low loader, we even waved them off, it's a good job they couldn't read Pats mind.

OUR FIRST HOLIDAY ABROAD 1981

Even in the hard times we had always managed to have a holiday, mostly, it would be Barmouth or Great Yarmouth. I remember one time we had spent two weeks in a caravan in Great Yarmouth, and as normal it was done on a budget. As the holiday was coming to an end we decided to travel home through the night, we thought it would be best as our two girls were very young, and the idea was to make them a bed up in the back of the car so they could sleep for most of the trip back home.

All was going to plan until I noticed, about 50 miles from home, that the petrol gauge was very close to the empty mark. This was at a time when most petrol stations would close at 9pm and it was now 5am. I didn't see the point in saying anything to Pat, as I didn't fancy the earache I would get. As we got to about 8 miles from home Pat must have noticed me constantly looking at the fuel gauge, as by this time, I could only imagine the car was running on fumes, I can't print what she said to me.

By now it was 6am and just 5 miles from home and I found a petrol station that was open. I still got quite a bit of earache from Pat, but at least it was for only the last few miles.

Photo, the girls settled down for the drive home.

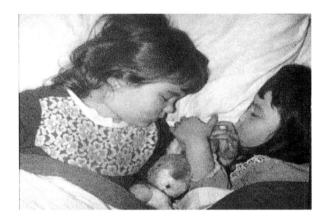

We had never been abroad for our holidays, but in 1973 Pats parents along with her aunty and uncle and her sister booked a holiday to Calleja in Spain, and they asked me to take them to the airport. I have no idea how I managed to get all 5 of them in my car along with their luggage, but somehow, with the help of a roof rack, I did.

I had just had an 8mm cine camera, so I took it with me to the airport, just to get some film of the planes taking off.

It was such a momentous occasion for me, as I had never been to an airport before.

When I dropped them off, I made my way to the observation platform, and hung around waiting for them to walk across the tarmac to their plane. I got a brilliant video of them climbing the steps of the plane, and then I also got the plane taking off. What a fantastic sight that was, the sun was just coming up over the Manchester sky line, and the plane making a magnificent silhouette against the backdrop of the rising sun.

When I got home, I said to Pat, one day I hope we can do that, but at the same time I wasn't too keen on the idea of flying. I couldn't get my head around how it could take off with all that weight.

It would be a further 8 years before we could afford our first holiday abroad.

Regardless of my fear of flying, we booked a holiday to Spain, it was in a place called Roquetas de Mar. I hadn't got a clue what this place was like!! Even though we decided to go in April, we were told we could expect some very warm weather, this was hard to take in, especially when we were used to England in April.

We arrived at the airport and I wasn't feeling too bad about the thought of flying, but we had our two girls to distract me. We got on the plane, Pat and the girls sat together and I sat in the row behind. Next to me was a tall stocky man, who later in the flight I found out was a roof tiler from Stockport. The plane started off down the runway and my nerves started to kick in. I glanced to my right (big mistake) I could see everything whizzing by, and the noise from the engines roaring didn't help. I was gripping hard onto the seat armrests, until everything seemed to calm down, its only then that I realised I had been gripping onto the roof tiler's arm. He was very good about it, and just said, are you ok now? If my embarrassment couldn't get any worse, Pat looked through the gap in the seats and seeing my face was a whiter shade of pale, put her arm over the back of the seat and said do you want to hold my hand. I replied in my best macho voice, I'm fine, I sort of half glanced to my left, and could see the roof tiler was grinning.

We landed at Almeria airport, and walked out into warm sunshine, and got on the coach to set off for our resort. The route we took went through some very poor looking villages, and after about 30 minutes our youngest daughter said in a very loud voice, "mummy, this isn't a very nice

Spain". I think a lot of the other passengers thought the same, as they laughed at our youngest's observation.

We eventually turned into the resort, and it looked magical. We were dropped off at our apartment and went to book in, the lady gave us our keys, then pointing to the lift, saying in very broken English, sorry, broke!!. The stairs to our apartment went around the outside of the building and we were on the 10th floor. With two big suitcases and two young children, we started to make our way up, but Pat has never been good with heights, so she was going up the stairs with her back tight to the wall and holding on to our two girls. The higher we got the windier it became, we reached the top and put our key in the door, Nothing, no matter what I did I couldn't open it, so, leaving Pat and the girls I went back down to the reception. Me, speaking no Spanish and the receptionist speaking no English, there were a lot of arm gestures, and I did what most Brits do, started speaking very slow and loudly, like, Key Not Open Door, the receptionist just shrugged her shoulders, so I repeated myself, only louder. Eventually, she took the key from me and we went up to our apartment, put the key in the door and kept rattling the door and turning the key until it eventually opened, she muttered something and went back down. The apartment was brilliant, a massive living room, a kitchen to one side and 3 good sized bedrooms, but the best was the big balcony overlooking the beach and sea. The next morning, I went in search of breakfast, with some pesetas in my pocket. I thought, some bread and butter, then we could have toast, this would be ok until we could sort ourselves out.

I walked up and down the road, but all the shops were shut, apart from a very little shop, thankfully the shop keeper spoke good English. He explained that the holiday season didn't really start until May, so a lot of the shops would be closed until then. He had butter but no bread, I walked up and down the road until I saw a van pulled up outside a hotel. In the back I could see it was full of bread rolls that he was delivering to the hotels, again, there were a lot of arm and hand gestures, until he realised, I wanted one of his bread rolls. The one he handed me must have been about 3ft long. I put some pesetas in my hand and offered it to him to take for the bread, he laughed and shook his head, gesturing he didn't want anything, so, breakfast was served. We made our way down to the pool area but as it was out of season it was empty, and the kids little pool was also empty, but I could see a hose pipe, so I started to fill the kids' pool. The lady receptionist came running out with what was now becoming the universal language of arm waving and finger wagging, but after some diplomatic shoulder shrugging and pointing to our two girls, and showing her my sad face, she reluctantly let me put some water in the kid's pool.

We decided to hire a car for one week, on our first trip out Pat said, shouldn't you be driving on the right-hand side of the road here, followed by the look!!

On one of our trips out in our little Seat Pander, we could see a horse running wild down the narrow road, heading straight for us, with a man running behind. I pulled over as far as I could, but the horse got so close to our car it took the wing mirror off, the kids just said, look mummy, a horse.

I was by the pool area, when I saw a couple arriving with their two young children and carrying their cases. When they eventually came out from the reception with their key, they started to climb the outside stairs to their apartment, I felt sorry for them, so with the universal hand gestures, I offered to help them with their luggage. They smiled and the man picked up one of his children and the lady took the other child, leaving me to carry both suitcases, luckily, they were only on the 7th floor. When we got to their apartment I put the cases down, and the man offered me some pesetas as a tip, I shook my head and waved my hand and made my way back down the staircase

About 3 days later, Pat, me and our girls were playing in the kid's pool when the family who I had helped with their cases came and sat near to us, and their children were playing with our two. The man eventually came over to us, and in perfect English, thanked me for helping them on the day they arrived, and apologised, saying that he thought I was a porter. He said that he only realised we were English when he overheard us talking.

On one of our phone calls to home, we were told that it was snowing back in the UK, and we were sunbathing. The day we arrived there was a card on the dining table, it had 4 different languages, the English part was offering the apartment for sale, for £3,000, including all the furniture. I often think back to that opportunity, and wonder, if only we had been brave enough.

Our first holiday abroad was coming to an end, and we explained to our girls that we would be going home the next day. They both got upset, saying they didn't want to go home yet. So, it had gone from our youngest saying, "this isn't a very nice Spain mummy" when we arrived, to not wanting to go home.

We had a brilliant two weeks holiday, and I was a very brave boy on our flight home.

Left photo, arriving for our first holiday abroad, Joanne holding my hand, saying, its ok daddy you're safe now. Right photo. Out for a walk in the sun, we couldn't believe how hot it was in April.

Outside our apartment, top photo, Joanne, looking cool in her hat and Pat giving Tracey a lift. Bottom photo, Tracey, and me in the kids' pool that I had to fill myself. The receptionist wasn't very happy about it.

WHAT TO DO WITH OUR ACRE OF LAND?

Just after we moved into our new house, we had the opportunity to buy an acre of land at the back, 4 years on and it was still a field.

One day in 1984 Joanne went and asked her mum if she could have a horse, she got a look from Pat that I knew well, followed by, No, definitely not. So, Joanne did what most kids do, if one parent said no, they chance their arm and ask the other parent. My answer was similar to Pats, but I tried to explain to her that keeping a horse was hard work, and would cost a lot of money. Also, both Joanne and Tracey were having horse riding lessons at a local stable once a week. I said that this was the best of both worlds, you get to ride a horse without all the hard work of looking after it. This wasn't the answer she wanted to hear; she kept on about having her own horse.

We thought it would be a good idea to show Joanne what was involved in owning a horse.

I knew a girl who had been in my class at school, and she now had riding stables, and lived about a mile from us. So, we went to see her, she confirmed what we had said to Joanne, that keeping a horse was hard work, but she did show us a pony that she was selling. I must admit this pony looked beautiful.

About a week later Gemma became part of our family. The first thing I had to do was provide a stable. I thought the best place was right at the back of our garage, but it would take me weeks to build. So, I thought I would make a temporary stable inside the garage. Our garage is quite big, its 26ft long x 16ft wide, so plenty of room at the back, and I could create this in a couple of days.

Tracey sitting on Gemma, the day she arrived, Joanne is on the right, and the girl in the middle is the daughter of my old school friend, who we bought Gemma from.

Before Gemma arrived, I had managed to build her a temporary stable in the back of our garage, and had organised a friend with a JCB digger to start to prepare the ground at the back of the garage to build a permanent stable. The concrete base was put in, and even though I'm no bricklayer, I had the concrete blocks delivered and started to build the stable.

One of our neighbours had also got a couple of ponies, and suggested it would be nice if all three could be out in the field together. This sounded a good idea, as he, like us, had bought an acre of land that was next to ours. We had only had Gemma for a week, when one of our neighbours' ponies had kicked out at Gemma, and we could see it had caught one of her legs and she was limping quite badly. We managed to get her into the temporary stable and called the vet. He arrived quite quickly, and after a thorough examination, said it was badly damaged, and thought, in his view, it would be best if she was put down. This, as you can imagine, was devastating news. I asked if there was anything we could do before going down that route. He said all we could do was to keep her in the stable, and for the first couple of weeks we must not let her lie down, as the actions required in her getting back up would result in her doing more damage. The vet said that all he could do was to give her regular injections for the pain, and hope the bone would repair itself.

I spent the first night in the stable with her, and she was such a good girl, she put her head over my shoulder, and that's how we spent most of the night. Every now and then I could feel her relaxing and the weight of her head resting on my shoulder was so painful, but we made it through the night. I realised that I couldn't do that for the next couple of weeks, so, all I could do was put her headcollar on and fix a tie ring next to her hay feeder, and fix it so it stopped her from laying down. We could see in her eyes her sadness, but the alternative wasn't worth thinking about.

We kept her like that for almost 3 weeks, until the vet thought it would be ok for her to walk around the stable, but under no circumstances must she be let into the field for at least another 5 weeks. The first time we took her back into the field she got so excited that we had to put a metal spike in the ground and tied her to it so she could walk around but not run. Over the first two months it was mostly Pat or me mucking out the stable, now she could go out in the field, it still ended up with us doing most of the work, and the vets bills ended up costing almost as much as we paid for her. I think Joanne had realised it wasn't just putting a saddle on her and having a ride, but to be fair we could only blame ourselves for not sticking to what we knew would happen.

It was agreed that we should find Gemma a new home, I went to see the lady we had bought her from, and she recommended someone who may be interested. A girl who was about 15 along with her parents came to look at Gemma, we explained what had happened, but they could see that she was ok now, and agreed to have her. They only lived 5 miles away, and kept us up to date with how she was doing. Over the next few years Gemma competed in many Gymkhanas and won lots of rosettes, and lived a happy and long life.

Pat and Gemma, in the temporary stable I built in our garage.

Gemma [laying down] in our field, and our neighbours two
ponies. It was the white pony who was the one who kicked
Gemma.

Below, the permanent stable that I started to build, but never finished before Gemma moved to pastures new. It would be a few years before I could find a use for it, but that's another story.

The next request from our two girls, was, could they each have a vegetable patch in the field, but not only for them, but also for their two cousins too, David, and Kate.

This idea, I thought was a good one, so I took my spade and went and cleared the ground, and dug four separate veg plots. I also built them a shed next to the plots to keep all their gardening equipment in, and it could act as, a bit like a Wendy house, so, they could play in it, and grow things at the same time.

Tracey, Joanne, David, and Kate, working hard on their vegetable patch. It wasn't exactly taking up much of our acre of land, but it kept them good.

After the girls asked me to make the 4 veg plots, it got me thinking that I should start to do something with the acre of land at the back of our house. I would sit outside just looking at this field, not quite sure what to do. I thought that it would be best to just tackle it in sections, so I started to put fencing around a quarter of it.

Both Pat and me weren't what you would call gardeners, we really didn't know the difference between a flower or a weed, so the easiest way was to level it out and put turf down, at least that way it would look a lot neater than a field. It didn't take me long to realise that I would need something a bit more than just a standard lawnmower to cut it, so I got a second-hand ride on mower.

Over the following years Pat started to take an interest in gardening, and I became the labourer, she would point to an area, and say, can you just dig that over for me!!

Tracey, [our tomboy] youngest, thought the field was fine as it was. She would spend hours with her mates just riding around it.

Starting to tackle the daunting task of levelling out just a quarter of the field. Just to the right you can see the Wendy house I made for the girls when they had their veg plot.

All the rolls of turf laid out ready to be put in place. both Pat and me had sore knees and an aching back by the time it was all laid. Our acre went right up to the skyline in this photo.

Pete and Sylv, who were our friends from Pats student midwifery days, got in touch with us and we arranged to meet up. They now had a young son, and we sorted out a weekend together in Blackpool for the illuminations. We booked a one-night stay in a B&B called the Reedley Hotel. Now, you may have to Google this, or some of you may remember a TV program, called Fawlty Towers, well this Hotel was like taking part in that TV program.

The bathroom was down the hallway, and to have a shower you had to put money in a meter that was in the hallway, it just about gave you time to soap up before your money ran out, so you had to put a towel around you, and go back out to put more money in to finish your shower. The beds were damp, and had nylon sheets, the shaving point in our bedroom was about one foot off the floor, and right by the door, so, to have a shave I had to get on my knees, and hope no one opened the door. At breakfast, along with the 7 of us, there were three other families, and the hotel manager, who had a striking resemblance to Basil Fawlty, would come into the dining room with one person's breakfast on a tray, then go back to get another one, and this went on until all 16 guests were served, but he would bring 2 breakfasts to our table, then the next breakfast to be brought out would be for one of the other families, but, we were British, and nothing was going to stop us having a good time.

The following year we booked up to go to the Illuminations again, but this time we went up-market and booked a two-night stay in the Norbreck castle hotel, it wasn't as posh as it sounds, but it was much better than the previous year.

While we were on our Blackpool break, we got talking to Pete and Sylv about our holiday in Spain. They had never been abroad and Sylv was very interested, but Pete wasn't too keen. I was asked, discreetly, by Sylv to take Pete for a walk, and try to convince him to join us on our next overseas holiday. I was successful in this covert plan, so, now we had someone to go on holiday with.

Over the coming years we would spend most weekends with Pete and Sylv, they would mostly come over to our house, and we would spend the night, talking, having a take-away and playing games like Trivial Pursuits. Occasionally, Pete would bring his guitar and the two of us would disappear into our sitting room, and leave the girls talking.

When spring arrived, the 4 of us would go down our local park to play Tennis, ok, we hit the ball over the net, not always expecting it to come back, but we loved it. To be honest it became a bit of an obsession, we enjoyed it so much. It went from just a Saturday, to them coming over on Friday, Saturday, and Sundays. We would play tennis, then have a take-away and sit talking, there were times when we would talk through the night and the birds would be singing when they went home. We got to know the park-keeper very well, he was well into his 70s and occasionally he would stand watching us play, I think he enjoyed laughing at how bad we were rather than the quality of our tennis. I remember on one occasion, we were playing in the rain, and the park-keeper came to us, saying, what are you silly buggers doing, come into my hut and have a cup of tea until the rain stops.

Pat on the left, with Sylv and our lovely park-keeper, with the tennis courts in the background.

There were 3 tennis courts, so normally we didn't have a problem getting on one of them. It was only when the Wimbledon fortnight came around and a few weeks after that, the tennis courts in our local park became very busy. One weekend we went down on Friday night to play tennis and all 3 courts were full, we hung around for about two hours, but it became obvious that because of these part time tennis players we wouldn't manage to get a game that night. The next day we went back down the park, but the same as the night before, the courts were full, these part-timers were spoiling our weekend. We gave up, and picked up our take-away and went back home. It was a lovely sunny night, so we sat in the garden eating our food, and as I looked up at our acre of land, I had one of my mad moments, and said, that if we can't get on the tennis courts down the park, then I would build my own, after all we had plenty of land. Everyone went quiet for a few seconds, and even though I couldn't see her, I could feel one of those looks from Pat burning into the back of my head, followed by, are you mad. The next question was, and how much would that cost!! well, I said, I could do most of it myself. Pat said, you have come up with some mad ideas in the past, but this is about as daft as they get.

I knew I would have to get permission from the council, and I thought there would be little chance of them allowing it, but to my amazement they agreed to my request. The only silly rule they put in was that the outside wire fencing should be no more than 6ft high, I mean, who only puts a 6ft high fence around a tennis court?!

I started to organise it, I hired a JCB digger, and with the help of my brother-in-law John, we cleared an area at the top of the garden, [I was now referring to it as our garden, not our acre of land] and dug footings around the perimeter and got a bricklayer to build a small 18-inch wall. Then I had the hardcore delivered, this was probably the biggest shock. We had it tipped on to our drive, and it filled the drive from front to back and was about 8ft high. Its then that I thought, what the bloody hell am I doing, all this for a game of tennis. The plan was to take the hardcore down a track that ran parallel to the far end of our garden, I was going to use my pick-up truck from work. After about the third load I found a car had been parked across the entrance to the track. It turned out that a neighbour who lived next to the entrance had decided that I shouldn't use it. I have no idea what his objections were, but he did everything he could to stop me, it became a cat and mouse game. When he eventually moved his car, I parked mine there, and just moved it when I took a load of hardcore down, but this was

277

slowing things up. This track was a public right of way and I had every right to use it, but our awkward neighbour wasn't helping, so I had an idea. I thought that if I put a road from our house up through the garden to the site of the tennis court then no one could stop me. The only problem with this idea was that the road through our garden would have to be 180 feet long [55 meters] to reach the tennis court, so, I would need a lot more hardcore.

This road, along with the hardcore, tarmac, and edging curbs, probably cost as much as the tennis court.

Once the road was in, it was back to building the tennis court, fortunately there were lots of friends who wanted to help. One of my neighbours said he could arrange the green wire fencing and the metal poles that would go around the outside. Even though the council said I could only have a 6 feet high fence, I took a risk and had it 8 feet high, after all this was normal for a tennis court. My pick-up truck had a tipper, so I was able to get the tarmac. I lost count of the number of loads of tarmac I fetched. I had a friend who worked for the council, and he arranged for the men who put the white lines down on the roads to come and paint the lines on the court.

Not long after the tennis court was finished, I was in our kitchen, looking up the garden, and could see two men going around the perimeter of the court, they seemed to be spraying some sort of liquid. I went to ask what they were doing, its ok mate, one of them said, we work for the council, we are just putting weed killer around the court. Apparently, they thought it belonged to the council, I didn't see the point in enlightening them that it wasn't council owned, as they seemed to be doing a good job.

Me looking a bit lost raking out the tons of hard core in the base of the tennis court.

Tipping one of the many loads of tarmac

Me on the right, finishing off the entrance to the tennis
court, with a little help from my friends.

The tennis court finished.

Our nephew Scott, thought it was perfect spot for him to learn to ride his bike. The fencing at the back was the boundary to our garden.

CALL THE MIDWIFE

AND FINGERS CROSSED,
THE A TO Z WILL GET HER THERE ON TIME.

Pat had stopped working on the delivery wards at the maternity hospital, and had now got a job as a community midwife. This was her dream job, she would see her expectant ladies at the ante natal clinic, then after their babies were born, she would visit them at home, giving them guidance and sorting out any problems or worries that the new mums may have.

The community job had its plusses, but as we all know, babies don't always decide to make their way into this world at our convenience. Part of Pats job would include being on call, so, she could do a full day on the community and then be on call throughout the night. The phone could ring at any time, and Pat would jump out of bed and rush to whatever address she had been given. Mostly on her own patch, she would know the area, and would make her way to the house, but at times the imminent delivery could be in an area of our city that she wasn't familiar with, so I would be dragged out of bed, and while Pat was getting her uniform on, I would be looking through the local A to Z to find the fastest rout to the address, [we didn't have sat nav back then]. As you can imagine this wasn't so bad in the summer months, but in winter, trying to find a strange address in the middle of the night on frosty or foggy roads could be quite a challenge, and add to this Pats sense of direction wasn't the best.

If the baby was to be delivered at home, then two midwives would attend, but if the mums could be taken to the hospital, then an ambulance would be called and Pat would have to leave her car, and go in the ambulance with the

283

expectant mum. Then she would deliver the baby at the hospital, after this she would try to get someone to give her a lift back to the house to pick up her car, head back home, and try to get an hour or so's sleep before getting her list of mums to visit the next morning.

As I have mentioned, Pats sense of direction wasn't the best. So, until she got use to the area, each night we would sit down and plan her next day's visits from the A to Z and put it down on paper.

I remember one day she came home, and started to tell me of one address she had found difficult to find. She had been driving around this big estate, looking for a certain road. After asking a few people, with no luck, she spotted two young boys, by now, not holding out much hope, she pulled up alongside them, wound her window down and asked if they knew the road she was looking for. She said they looked shocked and a little sheepish, then she noticed one of the boys was carrying the actual street sign under his arm, and was able to direct Pat to the road. You may think I'm making this up, but it's a true story.

Pat, occasionally would have a student midwife who would accompany her on home visits. On one of these visits, Pat was checking that mum and her new baby were coping, and there were procedures that had to be followed, like weighing the baby and making sure the new arrival was taking its milk. The student was there to observe, but at the start of these checks the student had asked if she could use the bathroom. After all the checks were done, Pat and the new mum could hear someone knocking, its only then that they realised the student hadn't returned. When they got to the bathroom door, the student shouted that the door was stuck, no matter how they tried, they couldn't open it. luckily the bathroom was on the ground floor and the student said she would try to climb out of the window, so

Pat went outside only to see the student trying to squeeze out of the small top window. Everyone saw the funny side of the situation, and the new mum went and got her camera. On the following page are just two photos that were taken.

Top photo, Pat holding the window open, and the student midwife squeezing through

Pat with the new arrival, and the student midwife on the right, after she had managed to squeeze out of the bathroom window.

I've said to Pat, that with all the stories that she came home and told me about her life as a community midwife, she should be the one writing a book, but I suppose the TV program Call the Midwife is doing just that. In fact, it has just reached the era in time, that was around the same time as Pat was working on the community. We are avid followers of this program, and Pat assures me that the story lines are very accurately written.

One thing that working on the community was helpful with, was it allowed Pat to get our girls off to school before work. We were very fortunate that the school that they attended as infants and juniors was just 5 doors above our house.

Both Joanne and Tracey were doing well at school, but they were like chalk and cheese. Joanne was so laid back she was horizontal, whereas Tracey was very competitive. On sports days we would all go to watch them. Pat and me along with Kath and Harry would all look forward to these events. We would see Joanne line up for the start of a race, she would be chatting away to one of her friends, totally unaware that the race had started, and not one bit interested as to where she finished, in fact in one race the rest of the competitors had crossed the finish line and Joanne was still chatting away to her mate. Whereas Tracey would be 100% focused, and would only be happy if she finished first. Tracey was the tom boy and Joanne was the pretty dress.

Tracey, in the red shorts, winning her race.

Joanne, third from the left. In one race she walked down the track chatting to her mate, and the poor girl who won couldn't understand why all the spectators were laughing.

Pat on the left at the start of her midwifery training in 1971, Right photo, just before retirement, with our grandson Oliver in 2008 who she had just helped to deliver.

THE ANSWER TO OUR PROBLEM WAS JUST DOWN THE GARDEN.

As I have mentioned Pete and Sylv would come over our house at the weekend to play tennis, but on Wednesday night Pete would come over on his own, and we would go in our little sitting room with our guitars. If the television was on in the living room Pat wouldn't hear us practising as we would normally play just our acoustics. Then, one Wednesday Pete told me he had met Geoff, who was interested in coming over and practicing with us. Pete said he was very talented, and could not only sing but could play many instruments, including bass and electric guitar, also keyboard and drums. It seemed like a dream to me, to have someone like Geoff to come and not only practice with us but could teach us so much. The following Wednesday Pete arrived with Geoff, and we had a brilliant night, he was so confident, and with his experience was soon teaching us new songs. The only problem was, that now, the noise, well Pat called it noise, that was coming from our little sitting room wasn't going down too well with her.

After about a month, we had progressed from our acoustic guitars and not only were we using electric guitars, but we also had a drum machine. After the lads had gone home, I went into the living room and got the ☐ from Pat, followed by, if you keep that row up every Wednesday you will have a divorce on your hands. I thought, that's a bit harsh, but at least we could then practice in the living room, and that was much bigger. [only joking Pat]

Top - Pete on the left, we would meet up most Wednesday nights and play our guitars in the little sitting room. I had got the 12-string guitar, so I can only imagine we would be having a go at Mr Tambourine Man, by the Byrds. It would normally be played on a 12 string Rickenbacker, but I couldn't afford one of those. Bottom - Geoff, when he joined us, our practice nights went to a different level. He was so talented, and a brilliant singer.

You may remember, I started to build a stable for Gemma, our horse, but she ended up going to a new home before I managed to finish it. It had stood there for over 10 years and I couldn't think what to do with it, but now I thought it would make a brilliant music room, and it was far enough away from the house to give Pat some peace and quiet on our practice nights. It was about 20ft x 15ft, so we set about finishing it off, all the walls and ceiling were made soundproof and I had a fitted carpet laid, it was perfect.

Above, making the old unfinished stable into our music room, having just put the new soundproofed roof on, with my helpers, we are all sitting on the roof, having a cup of tea.

293

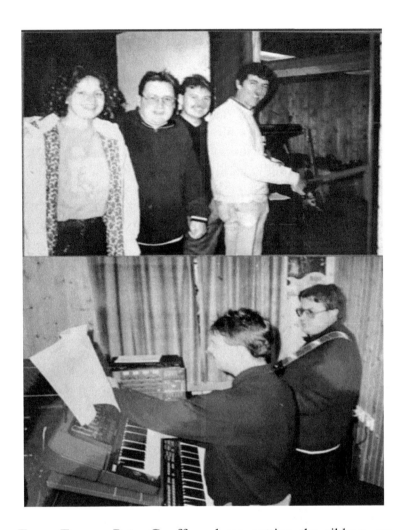

Top - Tracey, Pete, Geoff, and me cutting the ribbon, on the grand opening on our first night in the music room.
Bottom - Geoff on the left and Pete, inside our new home. Pat was very happy; we had moved out of our sitting room on practice nights, and we were very happy we could make as much noise as we liked without getting the □ from Pat.

Over the coming weeks we started to add to our musical collection with a set of drums, and special effects peddles for our guitars, and microphones. The problem now was, there were only 3 of us, and you can only play one instrument at a time, so our next purchase was a 4-track recording machine, this allowed us to record things like guitars and drums on the machine and then play along to them. It was starting to look like a proper recording studio.

I remember back in the early 60s, the Beatles had only a 2 track recording machine at Abbey Road studios, so you can see, now with a 4 track, it was quite a step up in technology in just a few years, but in 2018 I bought a recording unit that allows you to record 64 tracks, and it's only the size of this lap top that I'm typing on now, also, it only cost a fraction of the price I paid for the 4-track.

One of my mates came down to listen to us one night, and he was telling us of this fabulous guitarist, that was playing in a local band, and they played in the working men's club that was just at the end of our road. He also said that he played the guitar riff to the song Jonny B Good, by Chuck Berry, now this did impress us, even as good as Geoff was, he said he couldn't play that riff. So, we went to the working men's club to listen to this guitarist, and when they played Jonny B Good, we were blown away with his guitaring. At the interval I went over to talk to him, and offered to buy him a drink. I told him of our music room, and that we were looking for a lead guitarist. At first, he said he had been with his band for quite a few years, and he was happy with them. So, I said, why not just come down one night and have a look, I found out his name was Daz, and I told him we would be there on Wednesday nights if he wanted to see our little setup. It must have been a month later when Pat came down the room to us with Daz, he had knocked on our door and said to Pat he was looking for some lads who had a music room. Even though he stayed with his band, he started to come to the music room and just hang out with us most Wednesday nights. He made such a massive difference to the songs we were doing. I did ask him one night if he would teach me how to play the Jonny B Good riff, he said he couldn't because he just picked it up from listening to the song, and if he tried to slow it down to show me, he just couldn't play it. I could understand what he was saying, because when you watched him play, his fingers were a blur and he never had to look at his guitar fret board, he just had a natural talent, and that's something you can't teach.

Daz, our new lead guitarist on the right, then Pete, me on the left, with my new, Paul McCartney style Bass guitar, playing down the working men's club.

Carl, one of the lads from work, had been with me from the start, and like most of us when we hear a song we like, we can't help but sing along to it. So many times, at work, I would hear Carl singing along to songs on the radio, and unlike me he was always in tune. I suggested that he should come down the music room one night as I thought he would be a good addition to our vocals. Up to now only Geoff was doing the singing, even though Pete and Daz could hold a tune they were never too keen to join in. The first night Carl came down, the other 3 lads were very impressed with his vocals, he was a few years younger than the rest of us, but he loved singing the 60s songs that we covered. On one of these nights Carl just sat on the drum stool and started to tap out a simple drum pattern to one of the songs we were doing. The thing that impressed us was he kept perfect timing on the drums. Over the next few weeks, he not only added to our vocals but became our drummer. So, now we had Daz on lead guitar, Pete on rhythm guitar, me playing the Bass, Carl on drums and Geoff would play the keyboards, I say keyboards, because now we had two keyboards, one placed just above the other and Geoff would play both at the same time, giving us a variety of sounds from each one.

In the early days before Daz and Carl had joined us, along with Geoff, Pete, and me, our youngest daughter Tracey would occasionally join us and play keyboards. She had been having piano lessons and then had had a keyboard for Christmas, I don't think she was too impressed with our choice of music, and playing with 3 old men wasn't doing her street cred much good, but one night, Pete's wife Sylv came down the music room and said as it would soon be her big birthday [40th] and she was going to hire out a community hall for her birthday party, she suggested we could play a few songs. We were not too keen on the idea, but she kept on at us. For some mad reason we ended up agreeing, so, we started to get a few songs together, at that time we didn't have a drummer, so, we put the drum patterns to the songs we would perform onto the 4 track. We had never played in front of an audience before, and relying on a 4 track to play part of our backing, was a nerve-wracking experience, we were hoping and praying the 4 track didn't start before us, or even finish before we had. Even though we got through the night without any problems, we said that we would never do that again until we could play everything live.

One other thing we needed to do before our first gig was to choose a name for our band. Lots of silly names were suggested, until Geoff came up with what we thought was the perfect name. You have to remember that we are from Stoke on Trent [the potteries] we use lots of clay to make the cups and plates, and the nickname for people who work in the pot banks was clayheads, so that was it, we had a name.

[The Clayheads]. I even had T-shirts made with the name across the front. It was quite funny that it was Geoff who came up with the name, as he was the only one who didn't come from Stoke, he was a very proud Welshman.

On the day we were to perform at Sylv's 40th birthday party we took all our equipment over in the afternoon, and decided to have a run through of the songs we would be doing. It didn't go too well, the sound balance was not very good, and the leads to our guitars were far too short. This may sound trivial, but we had to be able to move around the stage unrestricted. So, I had to rush to the music shop in town before they closed to get longer leads. All these little things didn't help our nerves, but there was no turning back now.

Sylv's 40th birthday party, and our very first time playing to an audience, Geoff on the left, Tracey our youngest daughter on keyboards, then Pete and me. I can tell that we were doing Twist and Shout. It had always been my dream to do this song, it only took me 42 years, but I got there. I don't know if any of you are old enough to remember, Tom Jones singing live on stage back in the early 60s, along with the screaming from the girls, who would throw certain items of underwear onto the stage. [knickers]. Well, we didn't get any screams from the girls, but our eldest daughter and her best friend Sharron, I must add, purely as a joke, took some spare knickers with them. and towards the end of our set, they threw them on to the stage. One pair landed on Pete's guitar the other on his head.

Carl, the last member to join our little band, he came to just add a little extra to our vocals, and ended up also as our drummer. One of my most memorable events that our band played at was our eldest daughter's wedding. As I have mentioned, our songs were mostly covers of 60s music. We performed about 20 numbers that night, making sure they were songs that we thought would get everyone up on the dance floor. About a week before the big day, we had a request by Matthew, Joanne's husband to be, asking us to do, Don't Look Back in Anger, by Oasis, a group and song that was very popular at the time. We chose to do this as our last song, and I must say, it went down very well, so much so we did it twice. The second time, Matthew and about 10 of his friends joined us on stage, and we did the backing and they did the singing.

At Joanne and Matthew's wedding, when they joined us on stage. We did the backing and Matthew and his mates sang Don't Look Back in Anger. Carl on the left, then Daz, and me on the right, Pete and Geoff are somewhere at the back, behind us for our one song only, group of singers.

My collection of guitars over the years

I just thought it was only fair to show this photo of Pat's hard work in the garden. While we were playing with guitars, Pat had moved on from not knowing the difference between a weed and a flower, to becoming quite the gardening expert. The only credit I can take is being the labourer.

This was the patio outside the music room, I did suggest that the flowers must have enjoyed the sounds coming from our music to have grown so well. I won't print Pat's reply, but I got the look!.

There were a few things that inspired me to put the events that shaped and mapped out my life's story down into print. Retirement is definitely a leveller, and a big mile stone in most people's lives. Instead of getting up, having my breakfast then heading out to work, I now had the time to do the things that I wanted to do. You will hear people who have retired, say things like, I don't know how I had the time to go to work. Well, in my first weeks of retirement I can honestly say I felt a bit lost, even though we have a big garden, in the winter months, it doesn't exactly demand much of my time. So, what do you do with all these spare hours of the day, that, we retirees are fortunate to have available to us. Well, we have been blessed with 5 wonderful grandchildren, who would descend on us before school, because their parents had to be at work. Then around 3 o'clock in the afternoon we would collect them from school, then they all would want feeding. I must admit this chore would mostly be down to Pat, but they filled our house with fun, laughter, and carnage. After they were picked up by their parents at around 6pm, we would both stand at the window and wave them off. Then we would spend the next hour getting our house back to looking like you would imagine a house should look like with just two pensioners living there. Then it would all start again the next day. It was now us saying, I don't know how we had time to go to work. At the very beginning of this book of memories, I said I was talking to one of our grandchildren about when I was around her age, and I got that glazed look in her eyes. Well, this was one thing that got me thinking, how I wished I had asked questions about my parents and grandparents, but by the time I wanted all these questions answered it was too late, the people who had the answers were no longer with us.

Also, there were 3 photos that I came across, I knew who they were, but I had no idea about their lives.

This is the first photo, my maternal Great Grandparents, Joseph William Hales, born 1870, and Lucy Hales, nee Hammersley, also born 1870. I just remember my mum telling me that this was a studio photo, taken while they were on holiday. My mum also said they were the nicest people you could wish to meet.

This is the second photo that made me wonder why I hadn't found out more about them. This is my maternal grandparents, who we lived with until I was 5 years old. I do have a few memories of my brief time with them. The story of the man with the funny hat, from page 8, was the only one I can remember with my grandad. He died when I was 4. I have a few more little memories of my time with my grandma, in the stories on page 14, but sadly she died when I was 5. My grandad was Thomas Alfred Hales, 1895 – 1954, he was named after his grandfather. My grandma was Gladys May Hales, nee Dean, 1895 – 1955.

Looks like they knew how to have a good time, this photo was taken in the Travellers Rest pub, just a very short walk from their house.

This is the 3rd photo, and is of my paternal grandma and grandad. The back of the photo says it was taken in 1912, I don't think they were married at this time. Also, I would imagine they were not smiling, because, looking back on many old photos, no one seemed to smile. They eventually had 6 children but their marriage was not a happy one. Their story can be found on page 4 and page 5. My paternal grandfather was the only one to live to a good age. I was never close to him, he ended up living a self-inflicted lonely life in his later years. He had a 15-acre small holding that was way off the beaten track, even though we did visit him, I never really got to know much about him. I was in my early 20s when he died.

It's these 3 photos and the conversation I had with one of our grandchildren, that inspired me to write about my life. I never imagined at the start that I would get to over 300 pages and over 75,000 words. I thought a few A4 pages would cover everything I needed to say but I do tend to go on a bit!

Looking forward from my last story about the music room, it's becoming obvious that the number of stories I have yet to tell would make one book a bit on the heavy side. So, I have decided to finish this section of my memories here in the mid-1990s.

If all goes well, I will put down the memories of the remaining years in a second book.

Before I sign off, I must mention 3 people who have helped and encouraged me over the last 12 months

First, our very good friend Vivien Jones, who has written several books herself. Without her help and advice, I would never have got past the first page.

Second, my lifelong friend of over 70 years, Bryn Jones, who has come to my rescue many times when this dammed computer wouldn't do what I wanted it to do.

Finally, my long-suffering wife, who has helped to jog my memory on many occasions, and done her best to correct my grammar and punctuation. What a challenge that's been!

Love, Peace, and Rock and Roll, to you all.
Melv Williams
Just A Bloke from Stoke!

Printed in Great Britain
by Amazon

24654720R00175